Women, Rice, and Beans

Discover Wisdom in
Ordinary Moments

Includes 5 Guided Meditation Downloads

Ana Barreto

BOOKS BY ANA BARRETO

Self-Trust: A Healing Practice for Women Who Do Too Much
There is a Higher Power Within: 28 Meditation Prompts
to Find Peace & Happiness Within
The Nine Powers of Women:
Awakening the Divine Feminine Within

PROGRAMS BY ANA BARRETO

Become a Stronger Woman:
Quantum Healing Through the Chakras
Finding a Greater Wellbeing in a Busy World With Meditation
Timefulness: The Art of Aligning Time with Purpose
Making Space for a Loving Relationship
Discover Your Purpose & Mission
A Crash Course in Confidence

HOW TO CONNECT ONLINE:

Visit http://www.ana-barreto.com for meditations,
classes, and inspirational content
Like my page on Facebook: @ana1barreto
Follow me on Instagram: @ana1barreto
Follow me on Twiter: @ana1barreto
Follow me on Pinterest: @ana1barreto
Send your comments, questions, and concerns
to ana@ana-barreto.com

Copyright © 2016 Ana Barreto, M.B.A
All rights reserved. No part of this book may be reproduced in any form
without permission.
3rd Edition, September 2023
Interior Book Illustrations by Pablo Chaves, except for
"The Willow" Book Illustration by Sarah Evans
Photograph of the author by Tyiesha Ford
ISBN 13: 979-8-9876158-4-3
Library of Congress Control Number: 2016912539
Blue Hudson Group, Rhinebeck, NY

To my mother, Aracy; my grandmother, Maria;
and my daughters
Isabel, Erica, Christine, Janet, and Cindy.

CONTENTS

I have come to understand that there are two types of lessons: One that you touch, hold, bite, and discard or use, and another that your heart discovers. In the latter case, you feel it, and it unveils like a tattoo of a lotus imprinted on your soul, waiting to blossom.

INTRODUCTION

Where does wisdom come from? When I was growing up, I thought wisdom was learned as it was passed down through the generations, from grandmothers to mothers to daughters.

When it came to my mother's wisdom, I could only remember her secret ingredients for cooking great rice and beans or the words she used in Portuguese when one of her children complained about the other: "Quando um não quer, dois não brigam." This phrase means, "Two people won't fight if one of them doesn't want to fight." That line was her morning, afternoon, and evening pill, especially when she wanted us to understand that it would be wise for us to remain quiet whenever our father argued, complained, or punished someone.

I hated my mother's "pill" and thought that perhaps women's wisdom skipped a generation or two. I used to stand for hours on the windowsill of our second-floor apartment and contemplate whether women were supposed to be "weak" and remain submissive or "fight" and be abused. I kept the room dark so no one would see my tears of sadness and disappointment.

I expected my mother to teach me the mother-daughter wisdom that would help me to live a happy and easier life, even though I didn't know what an "easy life" looked like. I just thought that if I had a better role model, I could have avoided my many mistakes.

One day, I had a brilliant idea: I could share the female wisdom women ought to learn from their mothers in case they have mothers like mine. I wanted every woman to know all the lessons my mother never taught me and that women must know. In retrospect, how naïve I was to think that I knew every insight women needed to avoid trouble.

It was 2013 when I began gestating this book. I had booked a reservation for a quiet place in Vermont and had a draft of my list of complaints about my mother's lack. I was ready to pour my resentment on paper when I learned that my mother had an accident in Rio de Janeiro. She was seventy-nine years old. I canceled my book-writing vacation and spent ten days in Rio, helping and consoling her. As I tended to my mother, love and compassion grew exponentially in my heart. It was as if the ancient women of the ages whispered wisdom into my ears and showed it to my eyes, hands, heart, and soul.

Each day that I cared for my mother, I began to understand her true wisdom more deeply. The lessons might not have been direct. She never sat me down nor tried to tell me about life. No, her wisdom was conveyed in her daily life, and as the memories flooded me, I realized that they unfolded like her cooking lessons in an easy flow of love.

Brazilian culture is centered on food, fun, and connection. Cooking was a big part of my mother's life and her mother before her. It was typical for the women to spend hours in the kitchen, cooking and helping one another, especially with the rice and beans we ate daily for lunch and dinner. Rice and beans belong on the Brazilian table like fingers on our hands.

I discovered that there's wisdom in the simple acts of everyday life, like cooking rice and beans. Everyone has their little secret ingredient that makes the rice and beans their own if they are willing to pay attention.

As I began to appreciate my mother's wisdom more, I also found a dose of wisdom in my grandmother's life. She struggled as an older, educated woman living in the impoverished city of Salvador, Brazil, taking in the wash to support her family and studying culinary arts to become a chef in the culinary arts. She built two houses in the 1940s and '50s before women had the right to own a home or bank account without their husbands' or fathers' permission.

FROM BRAZIL TO NEW YORK

I am Brazilian. I was born in Ipanema, an area in Rio de Janeiro that most people recognize because of

Antonio Carlos Jobim's famous song "The Girl from Ipanema."

I left Rio de Janeiro in May 1988 with plans to stay in New York for only six months, make some money, and improve my English. Oh, and also to secretly reconnect with a guy.

But as is true for most of us, my life had its own plans. Thirty-five years later, I'm still in New York. I've lived in New York longer than I've lived in Brazil. In those thirty-five years, I earned three college degrees, got married, inherited three stepdaughters, birthed two daughters, got divorced, opened my own business, nearly went bankrupt, moved nine times (not at all typical for a Brazilian), traveled a lot, dated too much (very typical of a Brazilian), didn't cook rice and beans every day (unheard of for a Brazilian), and found a spiritual path. And it all started because of a guy who stopped calling.

I'm the third of six children unless you add the children my father had before his life with my mother. In that case, I'm the seventh of ten children. I grew up on an island off the coast of Rio de Janeiro called Ilha do Governador (Governor's Island), which now houses the international airport. This was before a bridge was built to connect us to the rest of the world.

My family was very traditional. My mother stayed at home, and my father worked. The only day we didn't eat rice and beans was Saturdays when we had crabs for lunch and pizza for dinner—except my father had to have his rice and beans, even on Saturdays.

In a traditional patriarchal house like mine, men made all the decisions, and women had specific household roles. Even mundane decisions, like what color to paint the walls or permission to go to a friend's house, were made by my father. Later on, when my father began relaxing his ways a little, he would send us to ask our mother. But she had been so well trained to fear making a bad call that she would send us back to our father.

By age five, girls were groomed to cook and care for their husbands. By age ten, my sister and I went to culinary classes to learn how to cook. I loved it because it was fun and got me out of the house. Meanwhile, boys did outside chores, such as shopping and taking out the garbage, and the women stayed home to cook, clean, iron, and sew.

My father was verbally and physically abusive. His authority was never to be questioned. The range of abuse went from yelling to spanking on Saturday mornings for being late from school the previous Tuesday. Although he became less abusive as he aged, his ignorance drove my plans to move out of the house. By the time I was fourteen years old, I wanted to leave, but I waited for my eighteenth birthday.

While my mother wasn't allowed to work and my father was self-employed, he did well for many years.

He purchased two apartments and a car and sent his children to a private school. I don't remember when the switch happened, but eventually, we became poor.

My father left the house every weekday morning at around ten o'clock and returned at about eight o'clock in the evening. On Fridays, he arrived home later. I didn't know what my father did for a living until I was in my twenties, as it was something we never asked or talked about. I eventually discovered that he had been an accountant without a formal diploma, a sales rep, and a partner in two businesses that went bankrupt when his two other partners stole the money. He then had to complete the remaining work that they left, all without being paid. At least that's the official story, but my father had many stories. It was anyone's guess which ones were true and which ones were not.

I'm sure my father did his best, but the expense of running a household with six children was enormous. So, bills went unpaid from time to time. We had the lights and the water turned off occasionally. Some days were feast, and some days were famine. My mother received food and clothing from our local church during the famine, unbeknownst to my dad. Other times, she borrowed money from friends to buy the food we needed or to pay an electric bill to get the lights turned back on. Occasionally, she used money from the hidden stash she stole from my father's pants on Fridays when he had some extra. No one in my father's household was allowed to ask neighbors for anything. He was too proud and thought people would put voodoo curses on whatever they gave us.

Most people outside our house really liked my dad. He was funny and highly charismatic. We had a grand façade going for us. Women loved his stories, and he could talk for hours. At least that's what it felt like when he encountered a neighbor or friend on the way to the street market, we went to every Saturday morning.

In my teens, I finally came to terms that my father wouldn't change, so I had to bide my time until I could move out of his house. That happened a few weeks before my eighteenth birthday when I was offered a temporary job as a switchboard operator in a four-star hotel. I told my mother about the opportunity, and she told my father. He said he wouldn't allow me to take the job because "only prostitutes work in hotels," so I left to go to my friend's house one morning. Then, I did the worst thing a girl could do in the Chaves household—I didn't come home that night. I returned two days later to pick up my clothes and left home for good.

When I finally found a home away from home, it was in Rhinebeck, New York, in 2005, a rural and historic town located two hours north of New York City. It was quiet but busy enough for my liking and known by Native Americans to be a sacred place, as I was told by spiritual locals. Of course, Rhinebeck has positive and negative sides for people who need to work for a living. It has the security of small-town living, near views of the Hudson River, gorgeous glimpses of the "blue" Catskills Mountains, piles of snow in the winter, refreshing early fall evenings, and long drives to go anywhere. My favorite part is the long drive home from elsewhere on the beautiful, narrow, tree-lined Taconic Parkway. That's when I have uninterrupted time for my thoughts to dance on the tip of my tongue. My best ideas were born on those drives.

MY MOTHER'S STORY

It was June 26, 2013, when I got a call from my sister-in-law, Flávia, in Rio de Janeiro. Calmly, she told me that my mother had been in an accident and was in the hospital, but she was doing fine. She said that my sister was with her, and my brothers were on the way there. They would call me later with more news. Flávia is a lawyer and the official "bad-news communicator" of our family. You have to appreciate those kinds of skills.

After three or four attempts to reach my brothers, I finally reached Marcus (child number five in our family), who told me my mother had been hit by a taxi driver while crossing the street after leaving work. She had broken a leg. At first, my brother said she had also broken a hip and jaw, but I later learned it was her leg and cheekbone. However, I realized that it was a nasty break.

My mother has a Native Indian name—Aracy. Her father named her after a famous singer of the 1930s, Aracy de Almeida, and also a granddaughter of a Brazilian Native Indian on her father's side. Born in Salvador, Bahia, on November 4, 1933, Aracy is now almost ninety and a widow. She's the mother of six and the grandmother of ten. She was technically retired during the accident but still worked because her retirement money wasn't enough to pay for her living expenses, especially her medical insurance. My mother had some savings, but not much, and spent her time going to work, attending church, visiting grandchildren, and talking to her childhood friends on the phone.

The main thing my mother taught me directly was cooking. By age five, I was helping her in the kitchen; by age seven, I could cook rice by myself. By nine, I was baking cakes with frosting made from scratch, in addition to beans, meatballs, mashed potatoes, and other dishes.

My mother learned to cook from her mother out of necessity, which was in preparation for her most important role as a wife. No one came out and said it, but we all knew we were "made" for marriage. The first time you cook perfect rice, someone says, "Já pode casar," which means, "You can marry now." Making perfect rice, a great cake, or delicious beans was clearly training for what was expected in womanhood.

Nevertheless, my mother isn't just a homemaker. She's a technical accountant who worked for over thirty years in a small firm, keeping the books and doing secretarial work for two generations. However, she only took this job when my siblings and I weren't allowed to return to school because our father was late with the tuition payment.

The school principal arranged for her interview with the accounting firm, and that connection changed her life. She didn't know whether people would give her a job, as she was already in her late forties and hadn't worked outside the home for over fifteen years. That interview gave her the courage to confront my father about returning to work. He threatened he wouldn't allow her back into the house if she went to work, but she did it anyway.

On her first day, she woke up at 5:00 a.m. to get the cooking done for the day and left the house at 7:30 a.m. She worked from 9:00 a.m. to 6:00 p.m. with one hour for lunch. When she left work at 6:00 p.m., she quickly walked to the bus terminal and prayed the entire fifty-minute ride home that she would be able to beat my father to the door and enter the house.

At home, my siblings and I were paralyzed with terror, wondering what would happen to our mother. We lived a full day in fear. We were so terrified of my father. I often peed in my pants when he reprimanded me, even as a teen.

That day, our mother managed to get home before our father, as he was unusually late for a Monday. That week, she got home one or two bus schedules ahead of him every day. During the second week, they arrived together one day, and we all thought the worst would happen. But when she got home, she changed her clothes, went to the kitchen to warm up the food she had cooked in the morning, and my sister set the table. We all sat down for dinner just like any other night. I cleared the table, washed the dishes, and went to bed. And that was the official day of the rebirth of my mother's career.

We heard from a neighbor that my father told her that my mother's job didn't pay much and that he had to give her money for the bus ticket. That was how things were settled in our house, at least financially. My mother paid all the unpaid school tuition, food, and utilities.

The original idea for this book sprung from my resentment toward my mother, which I discovered during one of my long drives home, but it has become something else. It has become a celebration of her life and love, with its successes and opportunities. I hope that you will not only learn from some of the wisdom I have gleaned from my mother and grandmother but that you will begin to notice more of the wisdom that may be hiding around you in the life of your mother, your grandmother, and your own life. We can find many hidden wisdom inside us that will bring harmony and love to our lives if we pay attention.

HOW TO USE THIS BOOK

Starting with chapter one, you'll learn the wisdom I have discovered during my journey. You will also find exercises that can help you unlock some of your innate wisdom that you can then pass down to your daughters or other young women in your life. I recommend that you take your time as you read and do the exercises at your own pace. Don't worry whether you complete all of them or not. This can be the type of book that you keep on your nightstand along with a journal and make notes as insights come to you.

I have also included some of my mother's recipes. Enjoy! And I wish you a wonderful and wise journey.

Chapter 1

A SPACE OF ONE'S OWN

The American Airlines flight arrived in Rio de Janeiro at eleven o'clock in the morning. My brother, Edoardo (my mother's fourth child), my nephew, Samuel, and my great longtime friend, Luis, were waiting for me at the airport. It had been three years since I had been to Brazil. I immediately noticed the traffic in Rio was worse than rush hour traffic in Manhattan. Without a car with automatic transmission, driving in Rio is pure exercise for your legs and a component to increase your blood pressure.

I didn't know the way to the hospital, so I followed my brother carefully in a rental car while remembering how to drive a stick shift in high traffic and not let the car die. (I wouldn't have been able to live that down in my family.)

I arrived at the hospital and parked the car in a crowded lot, wondering how to get it out without scratching it or the car next to it. By coincidence, my sister was in the hospital lobby talking on her phone with someone. When she saw me, she ended the conversation and said, "Ooooi!" In Brazil, this is a typical warm hello to someone you haven't seen in a while. We kissed and hugged.

"Mother isn't doing well," she told me. "She can only have one visitor at a time." My sister-in-law was already there. We told the receptionist that I would be the replacement.

When I walked into the room, I connected with my mother's look of "*saudade*." Unfortunately, there's no translation for this word. The best way I can describe it is the endearing feeling of missing someone. For people who don't know the Portuguese language, the word "saudade" may seem sad, but it is a happy one. Imagine the dance of two loves reuniting in space. That's "saudade."

My mother had the loving air of motherhood on her face, combined with the sorrow of what she was going through. "I'm so sorry! I didn't see the car. I didn't see the car. I really didn't," were her first words, expressing that she did something wrong.

"It happens," I responded. "Who knows God's plan?" I hugged her and caressed her pale face and unbrushed hair.

Before leaving, my sister-in-law gave me instructions for keeping the air conditioning on high, where to find the extra bedding, how to call the nurse, how and when to give water to my mother, and so on.

I spent that afternoon feeding my mother lunch, snacks, and later dinner—just like you would feed a child. I applied lotion to her back to avoid skin rashes, changed her diaper because the nurses took too long, and watched a religious channel on TV with her. We made small talk to keep her spirits up.

By the time night arrived and I realized I was going to sleep there, the nurses told me I had to have my own linens. The hospital had removed the one on the spare bed. It was too late to get anyone to bring me what I needed, so I used my travel pillow and covered myself with the bedcover my sister had brought in case my mother got cold. The room had a night light that was too bright for my taste, so sleep wasn't easy.

The first night I spent in the hospital was difficult for my mother and me. When the first nurse checkup happened at night, she knocked on the door and immediately walked in, turning on the lights. I woke up not knowing where I was. *What a jerk*, I thought. *Don't they know that the body recovers during deep sleep? Let my mother sleep! Let me sleep, too.*

The morning arrived slowly, with the nurses knocking on the door, announcing their arrival every hour. It was a respectful way to enter the room, but the hourly knock on the door can drive you to madness while sleeping. I wasn't prepared to see my mother so quiet, sad, disoriented, confused, in pain, and feeling guilty for inconveniencing others. But I realized there's no way to prepare for seeing the destabilization of your seventy-nine-year-old mother, especially when only forty-eight hours earlier, she had the ambition to defy her children and continue to live alone. Suddenly, she couldn't even brush her own hair.

Our conversations in the few weeks and months before her accident were about not living with her children. She had received an eviction notice from the real-estate office because her house would be demolished to make room for a new highway to ease the traffic in Rio during the 2015 World Cup and 2016 Olympic Games. Those two world events created a high demand for housing and drove rental prices up.

My mother had been unable to find an affordable place to rent and was pressured by my siblings to move in with one of them. She wanted her independence, her space, and her peace. On the morning of her accident, she and my sister had signed a rental agreement for an apartment near my sister that was more affordable with my financial help.

Later in the afternoon, I answered my brother's phone. It was a call from the realty company managing the house where my mother lived. They wanted to let her know she had two weeks to vacate the property. I told them about her accident and that she would have a second surgery the following day. Unfamiliar with the rental laws in Brazil, I asked about my mother's rights under the circumstances. The woman on the phone was patient but politely asked to have my brother return her call since he was the one dealing with the contract. My mother and brother had been notified nine months earlier about the eviction.

My mother heard the conversation and expressed her worry about where she would live and what would happen to her belongings. "Não se preocupe," I told her, which means "don't worry." But I knew she'd worry anyway.

The doctor told us that my mother would need to be off her feet for two months after the leg surgery, followed by up to four months of physical therapy. It would cause her to be out of work for about six months, but she needed the money from her job to supplement the expense of a higher rent since the rent prices had gone up drastically when Rio announced it was hosting the two major world events. Also, my mother's boss had already told my sister that he wouldn't allow my mother to continue to work after she recovered from the accident. My mother's boss seemed to allow her to work out of courtesy, but it ended then. We knew she would move in with my sister because she had the space and time to help my mother. So this was my way of preparing her for the inevitable and helping her see that she might not be able to live alone, or at least temporarily.

"What about my things?" she asked.

"We can put them in storage," I replied. "We need to cancel the new rental contract, and after you recover, we can start looking for an apartment again for you to live alone." My sister had already called to cancel the contract and get her deposit back.

That night, my brother Marcus arrived and told us the storage arrangements would be too expensive. I tried to change the subject, but it was too late. My mother's face showed her disappointment and worry. Her blood pressure went up, and refused to subside for the rest of the evening.

My mother had suffered a history of housing problems since she had moved in with my father. Much of the time, they lived with friends or in places that were too small. They were evicted more than once for not paying the mortgage or rent. They once lost all their belongings because they couldn't afford to pay a storage company. And now, two weeks after her surgery, she would have to vacate her house because it would be demolished.

I remembered Louise Hay's book, *You Can Heal Your Life*, in which she suggests that the emotional component behind high blood pressure is difficulty disconnecting from the past. At ten o'clock that night, the nurse advised us that my mother couldn't undergo surgery with her blood pressure so high. I realized that my own blood pressure was high, too. I recognized the telltale sign of discomfort on the left side of my neck.

"Relax, Dona Aracy," the nurse said to my mother.

"Don't worry," I said to my mother. "If we can't store your things, we'll sell them all and buy everything new. A new beginning! Where is the faith that you've always had in God? I'm here to resolve the house situation. I know you want your own space and your things. I'll do my best for you."

"Falar é facil, fazer é difícil" is a Portuguese saying that means "easier said than done." My mother used it a lot when I was growing up. In my mother's house, the furniture, the curtains, and the wall colors—all of it—had been chosen by my father, not her. She didn't even pick the towels she washed or the clothes she wore to church until my father passed away. She had long silenced her voice "para não haver zuada"— to avoid a riot.

OUR OWN SPACE

I felt so much of my mother's pain. It reminded me of Virginia Woolf's words in her essay, *A Room of One's Own*: "Women must have a room of one's own." She was referring to the feminine desire to be a writer. Still, I thought about how women need a room, a space, or a house of their own to pray, laugh, cry, meditate, retreat, sleep, orgasm, read, cook, decorate, mature, and inebriate with their own energy. It's a space of self-rescue. This was the first wisdom I gleaned from observing my mother's life:

"Every woman needs a space of her own."

If you have a chance to visit New York, take a short ride to Hyde Park and visit Eleanor Roosevelt's home, which is now a National Historic Site. It's the space Eleanor founded after "wanting" a space of her own for forty-two years while she lived in her mother-in-law's home.

Franklin D. Roosevelt apparently encouraged his wife to secure her own property to develop her thoughts. Some people also say he needed freedom from her supervision to explore younger pastures. Whether true or not, it was the only property Eleanor owned. She said, "The greatest thing I have learned is how good it is to come home again." Hyde Park is a great secluded place to walk and be with nature.

Another home to visit is Louisa May Alcott's house in Concord, Massachusetts. The room where she wrote *Little Women* is in her father's house, and you can see the small wood desk circa 1877, built by her dad. Even though she didn't have a whole house, she had a room of her own—a space where she found the energy and momentum to build her dreams and create beautiful stories in which women were empowered ahead of their time. You don't need a big house to find your own space.

All you need is "um cantinho"—a small corner and a desire.

HOW TO FIND AND CREATE A SPACE OF YOUR OWN

Creating a space of your own is a three-step process: find, clear, and bless it. Your space can be within the house where you already live, the bedroom where you sleep, an empty room in a house, a chair on the balcony, a bench in the backyard, or a corner in any room. There's no need to proclaim to the world that this is your special space (unless that's the only way to keep others out of it). Just claim it as your own.

Find it. When you can be alone and uninterrupted for 15–20 minutes, select a chair, cushion, or spot of grass and sit comfortably. Close your eyes and take a deep breath to connect with your spirit. Breathe in deeply through your nose and out through your mouth. This is how you open the connection with your heart. Breathe deeply twice more, and on the third time, hold your breath for 9–10 seconds. Then, release all the breath out of your mouth. Hold your arms out with your palms facing up, and declare out loud that it's your intention to find a sacred space of your own. "Today, I ask the spirits of light (God or whatever higher source you believe) to help me locate my sacred space."

Get up and walk around the room or house, looking at every area and corner. Trust that your intuition will lead you to the right place. Don't second-guess yourself. It's important that you listen to the first voice or thought you hear or feel. Just trust your intuition. Usually, the moment you ask to locate the space, a space pops into your mind.

Clear it. This step may take thirty minutes or up to two days, depending on the current condition of the space you've selected, the size of the room, and what you decide you want to do with it. You can count on at least two days if you're cleaning and clearing an entire house or floor. If you're working on one room at a time, and the space is already cleaned, it might only take thirty minutes. If you're moving into a new home, I strongly recommend that you do the cleaning and clearing before the moving truck arrives.

Perform a thorough cleaning by moving the furniture, dusting, opening the windows and cleaning them, scrubbing the floors, wiping the walls, and removing clutter. Try to find another place for the items, such as magazines, books, and clothes. Decluttering is important. That means removing an excessive amount of objects from the room. You may want to paint the walls, but this isn't necessary. (If you decide to paint, see the color chart below to help you select a color that will support your new intentions.)

Colors That Support Our Intentions:

Love	Pink, red, or green
Career	Light blue or gray
Finance	Green or purple
Health	Yellow or purple
Family	Green or light blue
Education	Blue
Writing	Light blue
Spirituality	Purple or lilac
Creativity	Orange*
Fame, recognition	Red
Tranquility	Shades of white or gray; light shades of blue; or light warm greens

*Avoid using excessive orange in the bedroom, kitchen, or entranceway. It can also stimulate addictions like overeating, overdrinking, and over-smoking. It's best used as an accent color to augment creativity.

Do you want to buy any new furniture for your space? It's important that you make your mark in the space by filling it with objects that you absolutely love and removing the things you don't like. If there are items that remind you of an ex-lover or other experiences in the past, it's best to move them elsewhere or get rid of them entirely. If you can't get new furniture but want something new to make the space your own, consider something inexpensive, such as a new throw or rug.

This step can be overwhelming if you have a lot of clutter in your home. Take a deep breath. If the clutter has been there for a while, you will likely have a difficult time removing it in one go. If you can't bear to go through everything right away, try moving the clutter into the garage or another empty room. Don't move the clutter into your bedroom, though. We spend so much time in our bedrooms, and if this space is filled with clutter, it will have an emotional impact on you and even interfere with your sleep. You can also ask for help from a trusted friend.

After you have cleaned and redecorated your space, it's time to clear the energy. This may seem strange, but trust me, it's a powerful step. Clearing the energy is a three-part process: action (body), word (mind), and thought (spirit).

- **Action.** First, you need white sage (strongly recommended) or sandalwood incense, which you can get online or at a New Age store. I also recommend a wind chime, Tibetan singing bowl, or bells of some kind. Blessed water (from a church or your own blessing) will work, too. These tools will help disturb the existing energy and improve the space with your new intention. Notice that I said these are tools that will help you. They don't do the work for you.

- You will need to connect whatever tool you use to your heart. Here's how you do that. First, feel your feet planted on the ground where you're standing. Take a deep breath, bring the tool close to your heart, and close your eyes. Now, visualize a cord running from your heart to the tool. It's an extension of you. Then, light the incense, ring the wind chime, bell, or singing bowl, or sprinkle the water as you walk slowly around the perimeter of the space.

- **Words.** Next, say your intention out loud with conviction and passion: "I clear this space for ease, flow, abundance, prosperity, and love," or choose whatever other intention you want to set.

- **Thought.** Imagine the old energy leaving the room through the windows, doors, and walls. Close your eyes and see the energy leaving as a fog, wind, or mist.

Bless it. This step will take at least fifteen minutes and can last as long as you like. After the space is cleared, it's time to bless it. Sit in your selected sacred space. If it's your bed, make sure you're sitting with your back straight. If it's a cushion on the floor, make sure it's comfortable. You may want to burn incense. Again, I suggest sage (light) or sandalwood (strong).

Close your eyes, take a deep breath in through your nose, and exhale out through your mouth. This will help you connect with your spirit. Do this two more times, and on the third time, hold your breath for 9–10 seconds. Then, release the breath out of your mouth. Hold your arms out with your palms facing up, and declare aloud: "This is a *sacred space*, and so it is. This is a *sacred space*, and so it is. This house is a *sacred space*, and so it is." Then, say your intention for the space out loud. For example, "I make the time and open up to hear the messages from my soul," or "I open my heart to God and connect with the divine spirit," or "I recover from _____ [*include your intention here*] and experience well-being," or "I love the ease and flow of my life." These are just suggestions. You can choose whatever intention is right for you.

After you have spoken your intention, stay there for a while and feel the energy of the space. Your mind may wander but sit as long as you like, savoring your new sacred space.

Visit the area often to think, meditate, read, breastfeed, or simply give yourself quiet time away from stress, children, or your partner. Keep the space clean at all times (as much as possible). If the area becomes cluttered again, clear it away as soon as possible. I recommend that clutter not stay more than twenty-four hours in your sacred space. Don't allow anyone in this space except those you have given direct permission.

Special Note. If you intend to remove the energy of a marriage from your space after a separation or divorce, it's best to slowly replace the mattress, pillows, mattress cover, and sheets, if you can. If it isn't possible, you can also clean the energy by using sea salt. Sprinkle raw sea salt on the mattress, and let it sit for at least one hour while you continue to clean the room and remove old pictures and objects that belonged to or remind you of your partner. Then, vacuum the sea salt, rotate the mattress, and make sure you use brand-new sheets. Donate your old sheets to a women's shelter or thrift shop such as the Salvation Army, even if they're expensive sheets with a high thread count! Trust me, they aren't worth keeping. If the relationship's ending wasn't traumatic, you could add sea salt in the washer when you wash the linens, including the mattress covers; I still suggest you discard the pillows.

Important. I have suggested removing and replacing these objects slowly because doing so too quickly can throw you off balance. At first, you will feel excitement, but within a few days, you will experience a strong "withdrawal." It will likely manifest a sense of strong sadness, void, and loss, even if the relationship was terrible. It's like changing elevation suddenly and getting altitude sickness. Your body isn't accustomed to it. Your lungs need to adjust to a new way of breathing. So take it slow. Let go of the items gradually.

Enjoy your own sacred space. Discovering harmony in your life will be an important part of your journey.

**Based on this chapter, what wisdom
have you found in your life?**

Chapter Two

LETTING GO

Day two in the hospital passed slowly. The nurses came in and out of the room to do their jobs, giving me unsupervised opportunities to look out the window at the beautiful winter sky and the lush trees in the southern hemisphere, distracting me from the Christian TV channel playing all day.

My mother likes the channel because she's a devoted Roman Catholic. She used to go to mass every weekend and often even found a mass to attend at one of the churches near her office. She helped in the church, went to confession, and took communion. She prayed every day, sent money to Christian organizations, went on retreats, read the prescribed Bible passages every day, and often watched mass on television. When someone told her about a problem, she knew a saint or a prayer to help resolve the problem. She knew that God is powerful and that everything is possible with God.

That night, before her second surgery, I remembered another saying she told us when we were young: "Há males que vem prá bem," which means "Bad things happen so that good can come."

"There's a life lesson to learn here," I reminded myself. I took the opportunity to tell my mother about my life events in 2007–2008 when I was working as a self-employed consultant and the American economy crashed. I had no business for months, and the little business coming in wasn't enough to pay all my bills. I was too inexperienced to realize that business would be slow from December to February. My life savings were paying the bills, and the next thing I knew, I was three months late on my mortgage payment. I received a note from the bank that they would take over the house even though I had made a down payment of 30 percent on the home. I tried to renegotiate the mortgage, but it was impossible with no secure job or contract.

With no money coming in and bills unpaid, I went to the welfare office and completed the application. While I waited to be called, I looked around at the people waiting for assistance, and I didn't look like them. You could tell that some of them hadn't bathed in days, and some were homeless. I knew I didn't belong in that room. I had three college degrees, a nice house, and a brilliant career ahead. When I got called and told them my situation, I was told that they wouldn't pay for previous utility bills and that I had to sign a lien on my house to receive assistance. I declined and left feeling ashamed, down, and hopeless. On the other side, I began to remember who I was.

I didn't want to sell the house, but my credit cards were maxed out. I borrowed money from friends, my ex-husband, and my mother without any other options. It still wasn't enough. I needed to sell the house to pay my debts. That night, I had a talk with God and decided to sell my home.

It took me two weeks to get the house ready to sell. I "re–feng shui'd" it and signed with a realtor, who wanted me to list it for less than I had paid, even though I had made improvements to the house. The realtor said the market was down, and homes in the area were taking six months or longer to sell even when their prices were lowered. I refused and held to my price.

The day after I signed the contract with the realtor, an open house for agents was scheduled, and I had to get the house ready for showing. I also had to stay out of the house for about four hours. During those hours, I visited a good friend, Gilla, who is also a great acupuncturist. I poured my heart out and shared my financial problems with her. She offered to do a "Tao" reading for me, using Chinese wisdom cards that suggest the attitude you need to have to handle a problem. My question was, "What do I need to do concerning my house?" The answer was a card that said, "Throw away what is spoiled." As she read the card and the meaning, I cried. Still, that afternoon, I finally decided to allow my house to be sold—physically, emotionally, and spiritually—without remorse, guilt, or self-blame. I felt lighter and at peace without clutching desperately to my house. This was a beautiful house with a pond and lake, but it was more property than I could take care of.

When I got home later in the afternoon, the realtor called me and told me that I had received an offer on the house for $20,000 more than I had paid in a down economy. As a result, I paid all my debts, and a year later, I bought a house for less money in a better location close to the children's school and convenient shops. By clinging to things that no longer served me, I had been holding up the arrival of a better future.

The following day, before she was taken to her second surgery, my mother said, "You can donate everything."

"Everything?" I asked.

"Yes, everything. See if your brothers want anything. If not, give it to the poor."

Her surgery went well, and she spent two more days in the hospital before going to my sister's apartment. That morning, I understood the second wisdom:

"We must have the faith to let things go to make room for what we truly desire."

THE CONNECTION BETWEEN FAITH AND CLUTTER

What is faith really? How do we know we have it, and how do we feel it? Is faith what we put into our marriages or our friends? Is faith what churches have been preaching for generations? These are questions people have been asking for centuries.

I have come to the conclusion that faith is trust in ourselves and in a power greater than us. Faith is love. It's expecting spring to come after the long, cold winter, knowing that our hearts will beat now…and now… and now…and now. Faith isn't logical, but it is knowing with certainty anyway. Faith is the secret ingredient that seasons our accomplishments.

People who have faith don't wait for what they desire because they know that what they want isn't missing. It just hasn't manifested in physical terms yet. They know about "divine timing," meaning things happen when they're supposed to. People of faith don't have to master patience because they have this sense of knowing. It's the rice and beans of letting both things and feelings go.

Looking around our house and seeing clutter means we're holding on to things, feelings, and thoughts that no longer serve us. Sometimes, the house may be clean and clutter-free, but we see a different story when we look into the closets, cabinets, drawers, storage units, and garage. Even when the closet is organized but stuffed, we can find items that we don't need and that no longer serve us. What about the wedding dress of a divorced woman? Pictures of old boyfriends? Newspaper articles and magazines with Thanksgiving recipes even though we haven't hosted Thanksgiving dinner for years? Those are signs of not letting go.

When you find physical clutter, you can be sure that emotional clutter also needs to be dealt with. It's like opening the closet of your mind and finding anger at work, resentment about a friendship, insecurity about your finances, unsafe feelings in your marriage, mistrust in life, and so on.

Simply put, clutter is a lack of faith in life. It's the belief that what we need won't be provided. We have to keep all sorts of spare things around to feel safe because we don't have faith that we'll be taken care of. This lack of faith is born of the past traumas that we've all experienced. Our minds justify clutter by saying, "What if I need this someday?" or "I don't want to spend money on an item like this again," or "I really like this." Obviously, you decide to keep things if it makes sense, but when there's clutter, it's time to be honest with yourself. Do you *really* need this or that or the other?

In my early days of feng shui, I was obsessed. I used to walk into my friends' houses and see a messy corner or room and know they were having a problem in the area represented by the room or corner. I saw the clutter or disorganization in the bedroom and later confirmed that my friend was having relationship issues that could have been helped by removing the mess. Of course, not everyone wanted to hear about that, so I often kept quiet.

Life moves us forward whether we want it or not, so letting go is important for completing cycles in our lives. Letting things, people, experiences, and emotions go shows that we trust life and are ready and open for the new. But faith is the secret ingredient that makes letting go easier. Faith is knowing that great things are coming our way.

WILLOW TREE MEDITATION

Letting go isn't easy, but here's a simple process to help you do it. The Willow Tree Meditation will help you release the emotional clutter and open your energy to let go of physical objects and situations that no longer serve you.

The recording of this meditation is available to download at www.ana-barreto.com/meditations.

1. Find a comfortable place and time where you won't be interrupted for at least ten to fifteen minutes. Sit comfortably with your back straight, if possible. You can select calm spa-like music to help you relax.

2. Take a long, deep, slow breath, and close your eyes to minimize distractions. Connect with the space by feeling the chair, the fabric against your skin, and

the air around you. Any noise you hear will take you deeper into the meditation.

3. Now, imagine or visualize a beautiful willow tree in the heat of summer. The tree is full, gorgeous, green, and large, standing in a stunning field. Breathe the air in the field and feel the warmth of the sun on your skin.

4. Look at the beautiful droopy leaves on the tree. The wind blows them so that they swing gracefully. Watch the birds flying by and caressing the leaves and branches of the willow.

5. Now, think of your career and any issues you're having at work. Perhaps you don't have enough work or are unhappy with your job. Maybe you're having problems with your boss or a coworker, or you are unemployed. Imagine that you pick up the problem and hang it on one of the branches of the willow tree. Let the problem take any physical form it wants, or it may not take a physical form at all. Just hang it on the tree.

6. Next, think of your friends. Bring to mind any issues you're having with them. Perhaps someone is angry with you, or you're angry at someone for not meeting your expectations. Maybe you have a friend who's bringing too much drama into your life. Perhaps your friend isn't there for you as much as you would

like. Place this problem on one of the other willow tree branches.

7. Now, think of your children or any children in your life. If you don't have children, perhaps your babies are your pets, book, music, or anyone in your life who's behaving like a child. It might even be someone who's ill and can't help it. That's OK. Whatever the problem is, imagine hanging it on a branch of the willow tree.

8. Now, think of your romantic relationship if you have one. What issues are you having with your partner? Perhaps you're thinking of ending the relationship. Or you're concerned about your partner's lack of commitment. Maybe it is you who can't commit. Maybe you're having fights or suffering from a lack of communication. Maybe you're sad because you want a relationship but don't have one. Take whatever problem you're having and hang it on one of the branches of the strong willow.

9. Now, think of any situations in your life where you feel you aren't being recognized for your contribution. Perhaps your boss, mate, or children aren't giving you the consideration you desire. In your imagination, hang these feelings on a branch of the willow tree.

10. Next, think of any financial issues in your life. Perhaps you're stressed by high rent or mortgage payments. Maybe you don't have enough money to pay your child's college tuition or medical bills. It may be the fear of balancing your checking account or consolidating your credit card debt. Maybe you simply aren't making as much money as you'd like. Whatever issues you are having with money, just hang them on the willow tree.

11. The next area has to do with your family. Perhaps you're caring for an elderly parent, or there's disagreement among your siblings about an inheritance or how to care for a parent. Maybe you are fighting with your mother or father. Whatever the issue, hang it on a branch of the willow.

12. Now, think about your spirituality and education. Look at all the "shoulds" you or others impose on yourself. Think of the pressures of going to college or the stress you have if you're taking classes. Maybe the problem is overcommitment in your church or spiritual organization. Or you want to have a spiritual practice but just can't find the time. Again, whatever the situation, hang it on the willow tree.

13. Lastly, think about your health. Do you feel overweight? Are you dealing with diabetes or high blood pressure? Perhaps you are avoiding a mammogram,

or your migraines are out of control. Maybe you have been diagnosed with cancer. Hang all these issues on the branches of the willow.

14. Now, in your mind's eye, step about twenty feet from the willow tree and look at all your issues hanging on branches. Notice how the wind blows the leaves and your problems as they hang on the branches. Allow some of the problems to be lifted by the wind and carried away. Wave them good-bye as they float out of sight. Make a mental note of which issues were taken away.

15. Walk underneath the branches, and imagine that you can actually walk into the trunk of the tree. Feel the effortless weight of your branches and the wind blowing at your leaves. Feel the strength of your tree and your connection to the earth. See people walking or driving by and admiring the tree with all the issues hanging on the branches.

16. Feel that you, as the tree, are strong and can let everything go, even as some of the issues are still hanging on your branches. Feel the calm, flexibility, and tranquility of the willow, letting everything go with each breeze.

17. When you are ready, you can open your eyes and return to your space. Take a deep breath, rub your palms together, and be present in your space. Make

sure you note the problems you were willing to let go. The next time you see a willow tree, feel free to touch it and thank it for the lesson it gave you in letting things go.

Do this meditation as often as you desire. It will help you let go and feel confident that you can handle the challenges of your life.

Have faith that great things are coming into your life! All you have to do is let go.

ADDITIONAL SUPPORT TO LET THINGS GO

Make a copy of the picture of willow tree that follows. On each branch, write down the names of the people, things, and emotions you are willing to let go. On the tree's root, write the experiences and emotions you want to grow in your life. Visit this page daily, or make a copy and place it in an area where you can see it every day. Be creative. Use colored pencils or pictures from magazines to make it your own.

**What people, things, or situations
do you need to let go of?**

Chapter Three

SELF-GENEROSITY

Getting my mother's bed into my sister's house was a dramatic event. Brazilians tend to do things at the last minute, but my family does everything even later than the last minute. My mother arrived at my sister's house before her bed was even in a truck. When it finally arrived, my brothers were arguing and blaming each other, which wasn't exactly what my mother wanted to hear two days after having surgery.

My mother had to eat special food and be medicated every two, three, four, six, and eight hours. She needed a wheelchair, diaper changes, special cleaning of her injuries, dry baths, dressing, undressing, assistance in and out of bed, and other things that popped up unexpectedly. I knew that my mother needed to be on a schedule and that caring for her was too much for my sister to do alone. We needed a nurse, but you don't find them hanging around the pharmacy or supermarket aisle.

Then, the wheelchair didn't fit through the bathroom door. My mother was too weak to get up from the chair alone and needed two people to help her in and out of the chair. She wasn't strong enough to stand, shower, or go to the bathroom without help.

It had been over eleven years since I last changed diapers, but after two children, I'd had enough practice. During the day, it was no problem to change my mother's diaper. Even though I was sharing a bedroom with her at night, she didn't want to bother me, so I kept waking up and checking on her. It was just like when my children were babies, and any little noise would wake me up instantly.

That first night, my mother moved while lying in bed with sounds of distress, and I asked her if she needed help. She didn't respond. Fifteen minutes later, I heard more restless movements and asked her again if she needed help. There was no response once again. At the third fidgety noise, I got up, turned the lights on, walked to her side, and asked softly, "Mom, do you need help?"

"I'm wet," she said feebly. The following night, it happened again, and she said, "I'm in pain," and the third night, "I'm cold." But she only told me these things when I got up, turned the lights on, and whispered in her ears. It was sad to recognize that my mother didn't know how to ask for help.

And with those restless three nights, the third wisdom arrived:

"Asking for help is not a sign of weakness but courage and self-generosity."

WHY DON'T WOMEN ASK FOR HELP?

Every woman needs help from time to time. When we lack the courage to ask for help, it's usually a combination of fear of disappointment, shame, and a false self-image. It's something we most likely learned from our families. It can be especially hard to ask for help if you're the type of person who is accustomed to over-helping others. This is the case with many women who don't know how to say "no." They live with the excessive burden of being supermoms, perfect homemakers, super workers, the best children, the best friends, the greatest grandmas, and so on. In addition to helping their families and friends, these women help in their churches, schools, local organizations, and communities. In time, some of these powerful women tend to resent the extra work they do. Often, the desire to help comes from a feeling of insecurity. We feel that we have to earn our existence, and we don't feel deserving of receiving help. We often fear that others won't come through and that we'll be disappointed.

But the truth is that asking for help is a way of being generous to others. It gives the people in our lives the opportunity to practice "acts of kindness," and it also allows us to practice "self-generosity."

You may be thinking, "Isn't generosity what we all practice when we donate old clothes, feed the poor, or give money to the church?" Yes, but these types of generosity have nothing to do with self-generosity. When we allow others to give to us, whether it's their time, ear, hugs, compassion, positive energy, or a diaper change, we practice both sides of generosity—giving and receiving. We give without obligation, pressure, or burden. We receive without shame or guilt. It feels good, and we all deserve it. And how about all those good feelings you have when giving to others? Allowing others to help allows them to experience those same good feelings.

When we fill our own pitchers with what we need, our pitchers have a chance to overflow. When we don't allow our own pitchers to fill, then we try to pour out to others from an empty pitcher. You can't give to others when you are bare. It's self-abuse. That's when resentment sets in. Generosity is a flow that needs to go in both directions to be healthy and balanced.

HOW TO PRACTICE SELF-GENEROSITY

1. Pour a cup of tea or coffee, and list the people you could ask for help if or when you need it. I know you're very self-sufficient and have most things under control. But make up some possible scenarios when you might need help, and think of the people who could help you. For example, "If I get stuck in traffic and need to pick up the children by

five, who could I call?" Make the list as long as you like, but try to have at least ten people on the list. Don't worry about what they would say, think, or do if you asked for help. This is so that you can see that generosity is around when you look for it.

2. Schedule something that gives you joy today. Joy can cure PMS, bad moods, stress, overwork, menopause symptoms, and fatigue. It allows you to slow down and pay attention to YOURSELF. I love going to a nice spa when I can, sipping tea in a comfortable bathrobe, and waiting for a massage while relaxing to the sounds of New Age music. But you can give yourself joy without spending a penny. A walk in a park may be all you need. Notice the birds and the plants. Recognize the following three keywords: SCHEDULE, TODAY, and JOY. If you don't schedule the joyful time, it's not likely to happen. If you absolutely can't schedule in joy today, schedule it for another day. But don't put it off too long. Write it in your calendar: a bike ride, a fancy dinner, a hike in the mountains, a manicure or pedicure (whether you do it yourself or have it done professionally), a yoga class, a trip to the beach, and so on. With this action, you're telling the universe and yourself that YOU matter.

3. Make a point of doing something for yourself every week. It might be as simple as sleeping in one day and asking the children to get a ride with someone else. Maybe it's taking a nap, going to the gym at lunchtime, or getting your hair done after work. Or it might be taking a long, uninterrupted bath with French salts.

4. List everything you do for others that no longer serves you. This can be a bit tricky because giving has probably brought you joy in the past. Usually, helping others does. The key is not stopping your practice of generosity but only doing those things that feel good without resentment. Once giving becomes a burden, make a decision as to whether you feel it's necessary or if you can let go of giving in that particular instance.

5. Ask a friend or family member for help, and practice detaching yourself from their response. Tell yourself that they have the right to say "no" and that it isn't a reflection on you or their feelings toward you. Maybe you want to ask for help with weeding the garden or moving heavy furniture. Perhaps you'd like someone to babysit while you go out. The goal is to become more comfortable with asking for help.

6. If you aren't used to doing nice things for yourself, these practices may sound overindulgent, but they

aren't. Just give yourself a small break and select one of the suggestions. With time, it will become a habit. You deserve it!

7. Humility allows us to receive help without shame, so practice on.

Where could you increase your practice of giving and receiving help?

Chapter Four

SOUL REFLECTION

Sleeping next to my mother in my sister's house reminded me of entering the physical part of motherhood in 1996. It was the first morning in my sister's house, and I felt just as I did when I brought my first baby home; I was tired and busy with a long, mental to-do list. But I made it a point to meditate every morning despite having a long day ahead. I got up and prepared my mother's breakfast, and I gave her a "cat's bath" using a sponge, a bucket of plain water, and another bucket of soapy water. I cleaned her wounds, gave her medication, brushed her hair, helped her get dressed, and got her out of bed and into the wheelchair to take her to the living room. Then I changed the sheets. My sister washed the sheets, and when they were dry, I made the bed.

By midday, I was able to leave my sister's house and go to my mother's house to move her belongings. When I arrived, my brother was already there packing. My mother had only been gone for a week, but there was a layer of dust so thick I could write my name on the furniture. It was disturbing to see the disarray my mother had been living in. After all, this was the same woman who made me wash dishes twice when I rushed through it or go back and sweep the floor again because I didn't sweep under the beds.

The sofa cushion was ripped, there were piles of newspapers on the floor, the glass top on the coffee table was broken, small piles of folded laundry throughout the house, and debris under the furniture everywhere. There was also significant water damage in the ceiling from a leaky roof in the second bedroom. (In feng shui, this is the financial corner of the house.) Of course, my mother has glaucoma. I wondered if part of the problem was that she couldn't see well enough to clean properly or had developed glaucoma so as not to see what had already become of the house.

I couldn't help but wonder, though, with four children nearby, why my mother had been living this way. I tried not to judge my siblings, but it was too late; besides, I was not around either.

When going through my mother's clothes, I found items I had given her in 1988 when I left for New York because I didn't have room in my suitcase. She couldn't possibly fit into any of them anymore. Yet, she couldn't let go of them. There is no question that the process of letting go is a very personal one.

After four hours of work with back-and-forth trips to my car with my mother's personal belongings, my brother and I left the house with the agreement to return in the morning, get more boxes, and contact a buyer to sell the good furniture.

During the long drive in traffic back to my sister's, I reflected on my mother's energy of "lack" that caused her to hold onto things that were too small, broken, stained, or ripped. She didn't use these things, but she felt she couldn't part with them.

Back at my sister's, I picked up each item and asked my mother what things she wanted to keep. By the way, she responded, I could tell she was upset. I could feel her anger and frustration at her situation. She was letting everything go without thinking, so I slowed down. These were her things, her life, and her memories. Calmly, with love and patience, I stopped the execution of her life (that was what it must have felt like for her) and reminded her that she could keep what she liked. This time, she chose the clothes, shoes, purses, belts, and sundries to keep. Before going to bed, I hung up all the clothes, color coordinated, and organized her new closet and drawers for her to begin a new life.

FENG SHUI

I have practiced feng shui since 2002 when my sister-in-law lent me the Portuguese translation of the book, – *Feng Shui: Harmony by Design* by Nancy SantoPietro and Lin Yun. The book was easy to read and understand,

and it helped me start a new phase of my life. Learning feng shui was like awakening the wisdom that already lived inside of me, and it was a natural way to express my philosophy of life. I became a feng shui addict and couldn't stop studying it, reading all the books I found in the bookstore. My thirst for knowledge led me to study with the SantoPietro and others later.

Feng shui is a Chinese practice older than time. In East China, houses and buildings are mostly not built without a feng shui master reviewing the site and blessing it for harmony and prosperity. The practice is based on the belief that everything is energy, and there is both "auspicious" and "inauspicious" energy. Feng shui is the way we create balance in every space by managing the yin and yang.

Feng shui literally means "wind over water." Just imagine the energy flow—wind moving over water with no obstruction. This is the way we want the energy of our houses, rooms, corners, offices, and lives to be—easy and flowing.

Imagine the wind (energy) over water (space) entering your house, but it becomes discombobulated, aggressive, or weak when it encounters broken items, old energy, dirty things, or clutter.

During my years of studying feng shui, I let go of many old and broken things and items that had no sentimental value in my current life. I cleaned the garage, the playroom, closets, and kitchen cabinets. It was an evolutionary process over months and years.

There was a particular dress that didn't fit me anymore, but I had paid good money for it and struggled to let it go. It took months for me to get rid of it. One great rule I learned from Jack Canfield, the author of Chicken Soup for the Soul and other great self-development books, is if you don't use it for six months, donate it, sell it, or give it away. (This doesn't necessarily apply to seasonal or special-occasion items like holiday decorations, tuxedos, and evening gowns).

It took me over a year to let go of all the little knickknacks, the gifts I didn't like, books I never read, mementos of old relationships, and so on. My mother had only five days to decide on everything.

As a result, I understood the fourth wisdom that I learned from my mother:

"Our home is the reflection of our connection with our soul."

MY HOME—MY SOUL

Every soul is beautiful, pure, and infinite. So, how can my small space be a reflection of something so big? Some people are naturally messy, while others are obsessively neat. Does it mean people with obsessive-compulsive disorder are more connected to their souls? Not at all!

Our connection with our soul is very pure in its natural sources. It is our thoughts and emotions that clutter the connection and create static. When we're centered, we can keep our space clean and organized. We're fully present in our lives, and everything flows effortlessly. When disorganization enters, we're able to correct it effortlessly.

When we aren't centered, anger, stress, or frustration prevents us from maintaining a higher energy vibration in our space. That's when dirt, clutter, and disorganization creep in and stay put. We can always force the reset button and clean the house every Friday like my mother made us do, but it takes a lot of energy when we're already feeling overwhelmed and depleted.

The easy solution people find to cope with the clutter is to ignore it, but the more we ignore it, the more clutter we build. The more we build, the lower the energy of the space becomes. In time, we become accustomed to the lower energy level and do not live consciously.

The clutter, the disorganization, and the dirt are minor signs from the universe that we need to slow down and connect with our souls. We don't need to drop everything and call in sick to clean the house. All we need to do is to make the inner connection to hear the voice of our soul.

When we ignore the nudges from the universe, life will push us forward, often in uncomfortable and challenging ways. I heard the universe will nudge a few times and then hit you with a 10 x 4. When the impact of a 10 x 4 hits you, like my mother, you will have no time to think. It will be sink or swim. The outcome is where we need to be, but it's much easier when we pay heed to the messages to let go sooner rather than later. Then, we don't have to be pushed into it. There's no need to suffer.

Women are naturally intuitive and sometimes find it easier to hear the voice of the soul. This is why women wake up before the baby cries at night. We tend to have premonitions. Men have intuition, too, but their left-brain dominance sometimes makes it harder for them to recognize the messages the universe or their soul is trying to convey because they need concrete proof. They look for logic rather than intuition, which some identify as a gut feeling. Left-brain-dominant women may struggle with accessing their intuition, too. People with this brain dominance tend to compartmentalize their world. With practice, however, it becomes second nature to listen to intuition.

Women and men use their right and left brains all day long; however, women tend to spend more time using the right side of their brains. This isn't good or bad. The key is to be connected with the soul and be able to use the right and left sides of the brain all day long, switching back and forth as appropriate.

All men and women ask, "Are all the voices we hear the voices of the soul or intuition?" The answer is no. The voice of the soul is peaceful, calm, and tranquil. It's easy to tell if you know how peace and tranquility feel. The voice of the soul doesn't push, fight, or judge. It doesn't focus on the problem. Instead, it offers guidance. It inspires and motivates. You will not hear a voice like that of a Yankee's cheerleader, pumping in this direction or that. When we make time to listen to the inner voice that comes from the soul, we begin to discern it from the voice that comes from the ego, with all its fear, anxiety, judgment, and busyness.

For example, the voice of the soul would never say, "Throw his clothes out of the house," "Call him again and again," or "Quit now." The voice of the soul whispers, "It's time to love yourself more," "You'll feel better if you clean the room before you go to bed," "Register for this class," or "Buy that book." And the message is always without demand or anger. The voice is persistent, but it doesn't pester. It is soft but has a clear message.

To hear your soul, it helps to create special dates with yourself to feed this special relationship, just as you would do with your significant other. Some days, we're too tired to sit and hear our intuitive voice. We have to carve time to welcome it into our lives.

In the past, people went to church on Sundays to connect with the Divine. Some did to buy a place in heaven, others to checkmark what society expected of them, and many to find relief from the burden of their lives. I'm not necessarily advocating religion; however, people made the time to be with God or a higher power than themselves. Growing up in Brazil, we knew that we "had to" go to church on Saturday or Sunday, and we scheduled the time. Before I joined the youth group, which was a lot of fun, I scrambled to attend one of the Saturday or Sunday masses. Usually, I bit the bullet and attended the first Saturday mass to get it out of the way. It was not out of desire but of obligation. The key to making room to connect with your soul is to "walk into the time" instead of "make the time." You only have twenty-four hours a day, and your superpower will not give you another hour to connect with your source, God, or what you consider a greater power than you. Your soul walks into your life when you're aligned with who you truly are. You can change your energy today and influence the energy of your house, room, corner, or office. This will help you create moments for the soul's guidance to arrive effortlessly. My suggestion is to be congruent with your space and elevate your energy. This chapter will give you some ways to do that.

IMPROVE YOUR ENERGY
AND THE ENERGY OF YOUR SPACES

Before you get a baseball cap to hide your unbrushed hair, slip into a coat to hide your pajamas, grab your car keys, and bolt out the door to get the things you need to improve your energy and space, you must know that everything starts with you. Yes, all the issues—the good, the bad, and the ugly—in your life were created by you. That's no reason to blame yourself. We all must improve our energy to create better lives for ourselves.

Know that working with energy is a process. But first and foremost, we need to be grounded. That's not the same thing our parents did to us when we were teenagers, and we weren't allowed to go out of the house for the day, week, or month. Being grounded is about being connected with the earth. It is feeling the nurture of Mother Earth, being and feeling supported by the universe, and knowing that all we need will be provided to us. When we feel grounded, we don't rush because we're aligned with time. We know that work calls can wait until Monday, the laundry can be done tomorrow, and that supermarket rotisserie chicken is just as good as a rushed half-cooked chicken you took out of the freezer in the morning. Walk into the time to be grounded and see (and feel) how effortless your days can become. I encourage you to try.

GROUNDING

We are all born grounded. People, events, and our thoughts about things, events, and people are the reasons we become ungrounded. Early on in our lives, our connection with Mother Earth is strong. Just watch young children. They go from being miserable to being unbelievably happy in seconds. That's because they're connected and grounded. That connection unlatches momentarily but automatically connects quickly and effortlessly with a hint of desire. As the child ages, the length of time they are unhappy becomes longer and longer as the child emulates the adults they see.

As we age, the connection is too far apart from the source. Desire alone can be enough to reconnect, but it must be a strong and consistent desire. The result is that we walk the streets of our lives very unhappy for extended periods; for some people, the long periods last for decades.

The key is to reconnect. We all need reconnection regularly; meditation is the best way I know. Even high spiritual teachers, such as the Dalai Lama, need and want to reconnect daily because they know the amazing feeling of being one with God, source, nature—whatever you want to call it.

GROUNDING MEDITATION

Many people tell me that they don't know how to meditate, that they don't have time, or that they can't stop the mind from thinking. They say that meditation is for Buddhists or monks from Tibet. But really, meditation is a connection with God, the creator, the universe, the soul, the divine spirit, the inner guide, and the higher self. Meditation is a prayer, a moment when the heart opens through the air we breathe, and we find a place where God whistles and everyone's hearts hear. Meditation makes us all ONE.

Some people meditate under pressure like penance, while others meditate with a vested interest in bribing God for winning lottery numbers or the name of their husband-to-be. Although all meditations are good, and any meditation is better than no meditation, unveiling the joy of the inner voice is subtle and profound. What we need to hear often doesn't come to us during meditation, but meditation trains the ear and heart for us to hear and listen. The wisdom often comes as an unexpected thought during a drive or when I first wake up in the morning, even before I meditate. It feels like that thought always lived within me.

For many years, I didn't trust that voice. Today, because I have a daily meditation practice, I can tell the difference between the voice of my soul and the voice of my ego. The more you listen and follow your inner guidance, the more it will come through. It's important not to use meditation like a crystal ball, however. It's a way to intimately relate with your soul, which is part of God—the All That Is.

There are many ways to meditate, and there's no wrong way. In later chapters, you will find other meditation practices, such as walking meditation, shower meditation, and even driving meditation. My suggested beginning meditation is to help you start the practice. It is short and will be easier for people who have never meditated before or are struggling with the usual resistance to meditation, such as too many thoughts in the mind.

As you begin a meditation practice, you will be guided to find a way to meditate that works for you. It would be best if you committed to a practice of some kind, however. While you can do it just once and receive all the benefits, a daily practice will help you bridge your connection with your soul and live an easier life. Don't be discouraged if you miss a day or a week or if you do well for a few weeks and drop off the wagon. This is a process. Once your mind connects with the well-being of meditation and you discover how centered you feel when you meditate, you'll want to do it more. You can start with a beginning meditation that only takes less than five minutes and then upgrade to longer ones.

You can download the Five-Minute meditation from my website at www.ana-barreto.com/meditations.

FIVE-MINUTE MEDITATION—FOR BEGINNERS

1. Find a comfortable place and time where you won't be interrupted for at least five minutes, but it can be done longer if you need additional support. Sit with your back straight if possible. Select calming music to help you relax.

2. Now, close your eyes and connect with your space, pillow, or chair. Feel the fabric of your clothes and the temperature of the air. Acknowledge any noise that may be in the background, but release it with no attachment. Refuse to let it distract you.

3. Take three long, deep, and slow breaths. Breathe in and out through your nose twice. On the third breath, hold your breath for nine seconds and breathe out through your mouth. Concentrate on your breath.

4. Now, move through a full body relaxation, one part at a time:

5. Relax your scalp.

6. Relax your eyes and the muscles of your face.

7. Relax your ears.

8. Relax your jaw.

9. Relax your neck, and keep breathing.

10. Relax your shoulders. We tend to hold stress in this area.

11. Relax your arms, hands, and fingers. Remember to breathe!

12. Relax your upper back and your lower back.

13. Relax your abdomen.

14. Relax your hips and buttocks.

15. Relax your thighs, knees, and calves. Keep your breathing slow.

16. Relax your feet and toes.

17. Place your attention on your heart at the center of your chest and breathe.

18. Keep "breathing through your heart" for a minute or so.

19. When you are ready, open your eyes, know that you are centered, and start your day.

GROUNDING MEDITATION—BEFORE WORKING WITH ENERGY

1. Find a comfortable place and time where you won't be interrupted for at least fifteen minutes. Sit with

your back straight if possible. Select calming music to help you relax.

2. Say these words out loud, "This is a sacred space, and so it is. This is a sacred space, and so it is. This house (or room) is a sacred space, and so it is."

3. Now, close your eyes and connect with your space, pillow, or chair. Feel the fabric of your clothes and the temperature of the air. Acknowledge any noise that may be in the background, but release it with no attachment. Refuse to let it distract you.

4. Take three long, deep, and slow breaths. Breathe in and out through your nose twice. On the third breath, hold your breath for nine seconds and breathe out through your mouth. Concentrate on your breath.

5. Now, move through a full body relaxation, one part at a time:

6. Relax your scalp.

7. Relax your eyes and the muscles of your face.

8. Relax your ears.

9. Relax your jaw.

10. Relax your neck, and keep breathing.

11. Relax your shoulders. We tend to hold stress in this area.

12. Relax your arms, hands, and fingers. Remember to breathe!

13. Relax your upper back and your lower back.

14. Relax your abdomen.

15. Relax your hips and buttocks.

16. Relax your thighs, knees, and calves. Keep your breathing slow.

17. Relax your feet and toes.

18. Now, bring your attention to the top of your head. Imagine a beautiful stream of light circulating about nine inches above your head. You can choose the color pink or gold. This is a healing light that will remove any energy that no longer serves you. This light is bright and getting brighter with each breath you take. Imagine this light coming down through the top of your head, down through your forehead, circulating around your eyes, nose, mouth, and throat. Remember to keep breathing in and out.

19. The light continues down your neck, shoulders, heart, stomach, arms, hands, and fingers, down the base of the spine, down your legs, down your feet, and comes out through the tip of your toes.

20. The light continues down into the earth, going down, down, and down until it reaches the earth's center. There, you will find a heavy anchor. Imagine

that you tie the light to the anchor with a big, secure knot. Keep breathing in and out! Stay there for a bit and feel the earth's energy.

21. Now, bring the supportive, loving energy of Mother Earth up through the string of light up through your toes, feet, and legs and up the base of your spine. Stay in this area where your bottom meets the chair. Feel the stream of light getting wide and leaving a bulk of energy there to keep you supported and safe. Now, bring the light up your lower back and upper back through your heart, shoulders, neck, and throat. Allow the light to continue up through your nose, eyes, and forehead and up through the top of your head into the sky. Take a moment to feel all that calming energy coursing through your body.

22. Next, concentrate on your breathing. You may start mentally counting each breath in for 1, 2, 3, 4, 5, and each exhale as 1, 2, 3, 4, 5, 6, 7, 8, and 9.

23. Stay there for three to five minutes, and focus your attention on your heart while you continue to breathe in and out. Know that you are supported by the spirit of Mother Earth and all that you need or desire will be given to you with ease and flow.

24. You may slowly open your eyes, rub your hands gently together, and stay there for a minute or so until

you are present in this space and reality. Now, you are ready to make some strong changes in your life.

UNDERSTANDING BASIC FENG SHUI

I already mentioned that when I studied feng shui, I would visit my friends' homes and find a connection between the location of the clutter and the issue they were having or about to have. The position of the bathroom or bed and the shape of the roof were more evident to me. I also found this connection in my own home with my own issues. One of my homes had a massive problem with relationships. Me and the two previous owners who lived in the house went through a divorce, all because of the shape of the roof. By the time I learned, I was already legally separated.

There are many ways to improve your energy, but my way is feng shui. This is a very brief overview of feng shui to help you understand the correlation of your personal space with areas of your life, to help you identify what areas of your home need attention, and how to influence your space with more focus instead of dissipating the energy by working with too many areas at once.

This information on feng shui will not make you an expert. If you are called to it, you can study independently, purchase books, or study with great teachers such as Nancy SantoPietro, Denise Linn, Lillian Too, Marie Diamond, and others.

But here are the basics: Feng shui aims to harmonize the space and create balance in the environment. It uses the five elements in nature or the representation of the elements to create a balance of energy in any space. This energy is called "Qi." It works to harmonize the yin and yang. It uses the Bagua (see picture that follows) to help people understand the nine trigrams representing the areas of one's life: career, helpful people or travel, creativity or children, relationship, fame or recognition, money, family, spirituality or education, and health.

Modern feng shui enthusiasts see some basic understanding of feng shui as common sense. Some of it is indeed common sense, while other aspects of it are more complex than that. Work at your own pace and level of understanding.

There are different schools of feng shui. I studied intensely the Black Hat Sector School (BHS), which was adapted to Westerners many years ago. I also studied the Compass School, which I use to help people with their own personal feng shui. I believe that the most popular feng shui school is the Compass School, which utilizes the directions (north, south, east, west), numbers (dates, distance, house numbers), elements (water, earth, air, fire, metal), and the form of the landscape to find auspicious positions for buildings, furniture, and objects that set auspicious levels of energy for the space.

The Black Hat Sector School also works with directions, numbers, and elements, and it also uses the Bagua (see picture below) as a map to represent the yin and yang of the space, as well as to impact the energy of the space that's connected with one of the specific areas of our lives. The main difference is that instead of using north, south, east, and west, we position the direction based on the front entrance of your house or room. Regardless of the direction your front door faces, the front door is always the lower area of the Bagua when we are looking at a house. If we're looking at a room, the entrance to the room is also one of the lower parts of the Bagua. If we're looking at a desk, the area through which we come to the desk to work is the lower part of the Bagua.

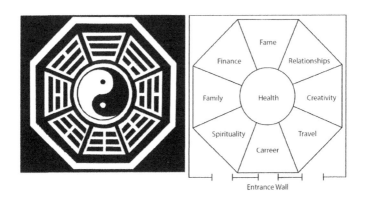

How to Use Feng Shui Bagua:

First, draw a floor plan of your home or room.

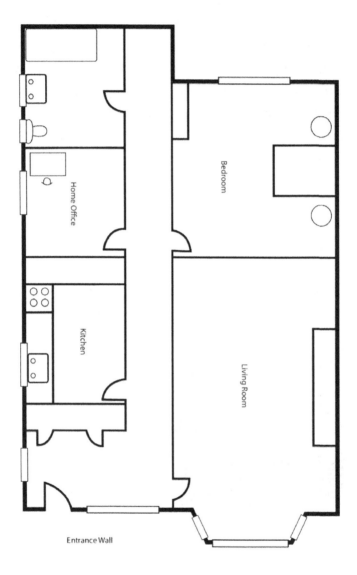

Bedroom

Home Office

Kitchen

Living Room

Entrance Wall

Second, locate the front door and overlap the Bagua over the house or space floor plan. Note the entranceway at the Knowledge area.

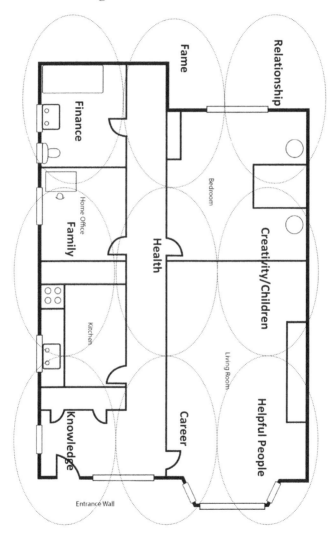

This is how the Bagua overlaps a bedroom or any room.

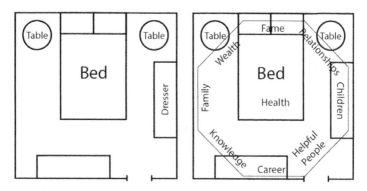

Next, identify the nine specific areas of the house or room to walk the nine stars to improve the energy and bless the space.

Tracing the Nine Stars

You will use this process at the end of an energy cleaning, which I'll explain how to do next.

ENERGY CLEANING OF THE AREAS OF YOUR LIFE

Now that you are grounded and you have a basic understanding of feng shui, you can get the materials you need to improve the energy of your home or room.

Materials. Cleaning products and tools, sage, sea salt, blessed water (you can bless it yourself), and the nine-star-trace process above.

Ideally, you want to clean the entire house, starting from the back to the front and top to bottom. I also highly recommend doing this when you move into a new home before your furniture and people arrive. If your house is too large, you don't have much time, or if you're always tired and not sleeping well, select your bedroom. If you're having money problems, select the kitchen. Select the office, entranceway, or bedroom to improve the work area. For illness issues, choose your bedroom. Cleaning the bedroom will also enhance any romantic relationship issue and all areas of your life if you sleep there.

On the day you decide to improve the energy of a selected space, try not to be physically or emotionally exhausted or angry, as you will likely leave this unwanted energy in the new clean space. Ideally, you should feel calm, centered, and inspired. If you already have a meditation practice, you'll know the right time to do the cleaning. If you're not at your best, you can try to do the grounding meditation mentioned earlier in this chapter to improve your energy first. Once you complete the meditation, you'll know if you've chosen the ideal day to take on the task.

Don't worry if today is not the day. Remember that feng shui is a process that lasts a lifetime. By forcing an action that you're not physically, mentally, or emotionally ready for, you cease to live in the present moment. In my experience, when I wake up in the morning and do my daily meditation, I'm immediately led to the area that needs to be cleaned. Other times, I start a regular housecleaning and find that I'm moved to do an energy cleaning in some other area of the house. I received guidance during meditation to clean a room, closet, or area, such as my desk drawer a few times. The "pull" becomes strong once you start working with energy. Also, it isn't necessary to do the meditation if you've done energy cleaning in the past. But I recommend that you do the grounding meditation every time you work with energy cleaning to make sure you're centered and connected to the earth's energy.

Now that your energy is centered, you can start cleaning the room. The steps I recommend are as follows:

1. Move all furniture and empty the drawers and closets. Then, dust, vacuum, remove spiderwebs, wash the curtains, and clean the windows. This is also an opportunity to donate old clothes you haven't worn for a few years. Remove excessive decorations, gifts you didn't like, and any items that no longer reflect who you are. Look at every picture and poster on the wall. Does it have a positive or negative image? Pictures that transmit loneliness, confusion, loss, or anger must be removed. Again, remember that this is a process. You may resist removing some items you know in your gut need to go. During my initial cleaning process, I had a Norman Rockwell picture of a sad girl looking in the mirror, wishing to be beautiful. I love Rockwell's work and didn't want to give that picture to a charity. So, I took it from my bedroom and moved it to the hallway to the laundry room.

2. Cleaning the Rooms

   a. The Bedroom—Relationship, Health, Finance

      i. To improve your relationship, make sure you rotate and sprinkle sea salt on the mattress with the intention of removing negative energy. Let the sea salt sit there for at least one hour, and remove it with a vacuum cleaner. Salt absorbs negative energy. You can also do this after you've been sick or if you have a good relationship and simply want to improve it.

ii. Change the sheets, pillows, and covers. Wash the mattress cover and blankets, and throw sea salt in the washing machine. If you're working to improve love energy to attract a new lover, replace the mattress if you can, especially if you slept with an ex-husband or former lover on that mattress. Only accept a used mattress from people you know if you can't afford a new one. The same goes for pillows, chairs, couches, and desks. Pillows are more easily replaceable, but your ex's chair and desk need to find a way out of the house. The sea salt will help until you can replace them. Also, if you can buy new sheets and a new bedcover, it will go a long way to improve the energy of the space.

iii. The bed itself and the position of the bed are of most importance. The bed should face the entrance door but not in direct line with it. (See picture of bed positions below.) The best bed positions are positions 1, 2, 3, and 4; the less auspicious positions are 5, 6, and

7. It would be best to have a headboard, but nothing that will overwhelm the person lying on the bed. Those very high and dark headboards have too powerful energy for a bedroom. Beds with footboards are also not recommended because they mimic a coffin. And no mattresses on the floor, please!

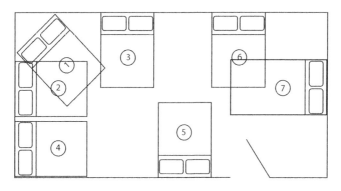

iv. To improve your health, you need a serious decluttering of the bedroom. Get the books, magazines, and knickknacks out. Try to get a new mattress if you've recently recovered from a serious illness. The energy of a serious disease stays in the space. Although most energy can be cleaned from a mattress, the energy of illness has many layers and will require the big dogs to move it out. Ensure the mattress is never placed directly on the floor, and nothing is stored under the bed.

For beds with storage drawers under the mattress, make sure you move the bed, clean the floor underneath, empty the drawers, and clean them. Please return the items that are still in use and are clean, and organize the drawer until it's only half full and not over-stuffed. Buy new pillows and bedcovers. Use the color yellow in some room items, but only if you like the color yellow. This is the color that supports health. There are many shades of yellow, and you don't want an aggressive tone.

v. Mind the wall. You don't want empty walls, but the art or furniture against the wall needs to support the intention of radiant health. If you have your grandmother's armoire, and she died of a terminal disease, get the furniture out of the room. If you bought the bed at a thrift store, check how you feel about the piece. Trust your intuition, but clean the energy anyway.

vi. To improve finances, follow the declutter directions above. Make sure drawers are not overstuffed. Remove any broken items, and create a comfortable and pretty space. You may want to use the color green or purple.

Again, I recommend you use the color you like over the colors feng shui recommends.

b. The Kitchen—Finance, Career

i. Remove expired food from the pantry and refrigerator. Donate food that you bought, but no one eats. Discard the excessive to-go containers, plastic bags, broken mugs, chipped plates, worn pans, etc. Clean and reorganize the cabinets, refrigerator, and freezer. Make sure there is room left for better items.

ii. The position of the stove is considered the key element for financial issues. Ideally, the cook facing the stove should be able to see the people walking into the kitchen easily. Pay attention to this rule if you're building a house or renovating your kitchen. If not, you can use a mirror to correct it. Keep the stove clean, and don't forget to clean the oven. Make sure you use the stove and oven occasionally and rotate the burners you use.

iii. Donate extra glasses, mugs, and plates you don't use, even on holidays. Remove excessive decorations, gifts you don't like, and any items that no longer reflect who you are.

Wash the curtains and windows. Make sure there is enough light coming through.

c. The Office—Career, Finances, and Recognition

    i. To improve your career, recognition, and finances, clean your office. Organize the papers, discard old bills (older than ten years), magazines, textbooks, etc. Remember to donate old books that no longer interest you. Clean all drawers and organize supplies. Remove excessive decorations from the walls and desk and any items that no longer reflect who you are. Your taste evolves with time. Try to keep the place clean and organized at all times. Ask yourself: "If I had a million-dollar client come here, would I feel comfortable receiving that person in the space? Does this space reflect who I am?" You don't have to spend thousands of dollars to make this space your own.

    ii. Your desk needs to be strong and reflect the image you want people to have of you. Like the bed, the person using the desk must face the entrance. Make sure your desk is fully functional. Replace or repair wobbly desks and chairs. The office space must be clean, light, and inviting, especially if you work long hours there.

   iii. Look at every picture and poster on the wall. Does it have a positive or negative image? If the pictures don't transmit success and happiness, find a new place for them or discard them. Then, replace them with inspiring pictures or messages.

d. The Bathroom—Finances

   i. The energy of the bathroom is a tricky one. In ancient Chinese tradition, bathrooms were not built inside the house. As time progressed, bathrooms made their way into Chinese homes, but they were hidden so that the Qi (energy force) couldn't find and take the finances down with them.

   ii. It's vital always to keep the bathrooms clean. (No news here, right?) But the key word is Toilet. Energy will easily follow the path of water. Because of the strong yang energy of water, we always need to keep the toilet seat down when flushing so that money energy isn't flushed down the toilet. It takes time to get everyone on board, but it can be done.

SPACE CLEARING

After cleaning the space, it's time to do a powerful clearing with the three secrets reinforced: body, mind, and spirit. You will use an Ousting Mudra hand gesture to eliminate the undesired energy. See the picture of Ousting Mudra below. You'll think of the outcome you need for each of the nine areas of your life, and you'll repeat the Heart Sutra Mantra nine times as you walk the nine-star path to support the clearing.

The Heart Sutra Mantra is, "GATE GATE, BORO GATE, BORO SUN GATE, BODHI SO PO HE." (Gate is pronounced Gatay.) This mantra is like a prayer loosely translated as "grant our wishes."

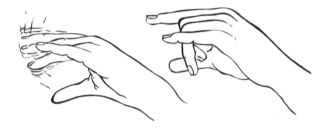

Light some sage, or get a bell or singing bowl.

Get the diagram of your house or room.

Get the diagram of tracing the Nine Star path on page 80 and locate the nine areas of the path in the space. You may want to walk with the book if you like.

Locate the first stop of the star path in the family area of the room or house, and go there with your clearing tool of choice.

Take a deep breath, begin by repeating the Heart Sutra Mantra nine times, and at the same time, do the Ousting Mudra by flicking your fingers nine times. "GATE GATE, BORO GATE, BORO SUN GATE, BODHI SO PO HE."

As you speak the mantra nine times, think about the desired outcome. For example, if you're having too many family fights in the house when you walk in the family area, imagine your family laughing and getting along. If you're on the health path (#3 stop) and fighting an illness, imagine your cells happy and healed. Feel the well-being and joy of radiant health. If you want to find a life partner, as you get to stop # 9, imagine yourself at the altar, feeling love and loved. I recommend that you work with strong intentions in only three areas of your life at a time. This will improve your focus.

Walk the nine areas.

Now, the space is ready to support your energy and the people living in the house. It will help you hear your inner voice and avoid getting pushed by the universe when you least expect it.

I have found that this process usually takes me a whole day as I take a break to eat, drink, cook, go to the store because I ran out of products, answer the phone, get distracted in another area, and so on. I like to shower after cleaning, admire my work, and only use the space for meditation at the end of the day, before bedtime.

Important. This process may disrupt your sleep for two to three nights. You may wake up between 2:30 a.m. and 3:30 a.m. after you do an energy clearing. The reason for this is that you have elevated the energy of the space, and your body's energy is used for the old energy, which is denser. Don't worry. You'll sleep better after the second or third night. Also, although you may lose one to three hours of sleep after a clearing, your energy level won't be impacted.

Do yourself a favor, and don't tell others about waking up in the middle of the night. This is not insomnia; it's spiritual progression! You'll probably have incredible insights during this time. Take your pen and paper everywhere, and write the insights down. Your intuition will be on steroids!

YOU AND EVERYTHING ARE ENERGY

We know energy as the electric current passing through the microwave or through lights in the ceiling. Science has come a long way toward discovering that nothing stays still and everything is moving, creating, dispersing, and transforming energy.

The bed, the table, the makeup, the clothes, and the cute $300 sandals you saw at the local boutique all carry energy. We are all very powerful sources of energy. Even our thoughts are energy. Yes, the constant mind chatter in your head about the kids, the job, the house, the rice and beans on the stove, the car accident, the house, and the traffic are energy. The gossip or good advice you give a neighbor is energy. The calm thoughts after meditation are energy. The music you listen to, the sound of the waves, or the jackhammer on a construction site is energy. The photos on the wall have energy. The wedding album and the credit card statements have energy and are energy. Yes, everything is energy. They all have tiny molecules coursing through them.

Have you ever walked into a store and decided to leave within a matter of steps? You perceived the store's energy, which was the opposite of yours. It doesn't mean that the energy of the store was bad. It just means that your energy and the store's energy were too far apart.

Energy behaves like water, which contracts and expands. It changes color, it nurtures, and it ends. It builds, and it destroys. Yet, it's a necessary element in everyone's lives. Energy is also like music. It can impact your mood with happiness or sadness. It can help you relax or drive you crazy. It can soothe you, and it can make you deaf. Our energy can contaminate or uplift the energy of others and the spaces they occupy.

Now that you know you're energy, it would be wise to know how to manage the energy within you and around you. I'm going out on a limb here and assuming that you'd like your energy and the energy around you to be supportive, nurturing, and helpful toward building your dreams.

YOU CAN CHANGE YOUR ENERGY

If you don't like the energy of the people around you, you need to work on your own energy. If you don't like the people you work, live with, or the environment where you work or hang out, you need to work on your own energy. You see, you can't blame them. It's you!

Don't panic if you perceive your coworkers as selfish, backstabbing, energy vampires, or drama queens. Yes, there's a chance that you have the same selfish, back-stabbing, energy vampire and drama queen energy in you. But it could also be that you've just become used to bearing that level of energy at home and other places of employment. If you aren't happy about it, though, change it. It can be easier said than done, but you're already on your way because you've brought it to a conscious level. You're thinking about it now, and the first step to making change is to know what you *don't* like. Then you'll be able to figure out what you *do* like.

For example, if you didn't know what darkness was, you wouldn't know to search for the light. You wouldn't look for high if you didn't know about low. Temporary unhappiness is a good place to start if you plan not to be there very long. Unfortunately, people get used to feeling discontent and stay there longer than necessary. But it's only a stepping stone away.

I usually give myself a few hours to vent and be mad. Then, I let go. If the issue is very big, I might take twenty-four hours. It takes practice. After you fully understand how that state of negativity impacts your energy and your life, you'll want to give it no more time than absolutely necessary to let it go. Just be patient with yourself, and know that it's a process. You'll get there if you want to. If you already know that you deplete energy by your emotions, you'll want to pay special attention to this chapter to learn how to change your energy.

MANAGING YOUR ENERGY

Some people's energy is very strong, others not so much. Strong energy is great when positive, uplifting, and nurturing, but it's far from desirable when it's negative, disheartening, or depressive. Nevertheless, a short dose of negative energy can be a catalyst for people to change and seek positive, uplifting energy. This dichotomy is the mystery of energy that we need to understand, practice, and master.

Also, the energy of your space will slowly influence your internal energy. Here's a way for you to know if your house is uplifting or diminishing your energy:

Wake up early in the morning and go for a walk in a clean, very green park for at least thirty minutes. Breathe in the fresh air and notice the flowers, trees, birds, animals, and sky. During the winter months, find space with evergreen trees. Before returning to your house and walking through the door, note your energy level by rating it from 1 to 10, with 1 as the lowest and 10 as the highest. Ask yourself, "What level is my energy?" If your energy is 5 or below, return to the park and take another 30 minutes. This time, make sure you allow the trees, leaves, flowers, birds, and sky to affect you truly. It's impossible to commune with nature for thirty minutes and not improve your energy level to at least a few degrees. This is a walking meditation.

After you complete the exercise, check your energy once again before entering the house, and find your energy level, which should be between 6 and 10. Walk back into your house and do your normal routine for fifteen minutes. Then, check your energy again. Has it improved, decreased, or stayed the same? If your energy stays the same or improved, know that you're doing a great job with your house's energy. If your energy level decreases, there's some work to do. Start planning your feng shui day for the near future.

EVALUATING YOUR ENERGY

Your energy will slowly influence your space. Then, the energy of your space will influence your internal energy. The question is, who influences what, or what influences who? The answer is both. It's a warm dance of tango—not a samba—that our space and personal energies engage in daily. Actually, if you find time to dance—whether a samba or something else in your house—you'll improve both your own energy and the energy of your space.

I recommend that you manage your energy first and then use it to transform the energy of the space. Here are some ways to help you manage your energy:

1. **Shower.** Yes, it's that simple. Our body is about sixty percent water. Water has been used to bless people in many different religions. It refreshes and changes your mood, which changes your feelings. A positive change in your feelings is the most important component of changing your energy. If you're feeling sick, take a shower. If you had a fight with someone, take a shower. If you had a bad day at work, take a shower. And wash your hair. Some women, especially Brazilians with curly hair, don't wash their hair daily, but your energy will change fast when you do. Feel free to use scented soap, shower mist, or body wash with lavender, vanilla, or eucalyptus. These fra-

grances help improve your mood, too. Baths will do the same as a shower.

2. **Food.** Colorful, healthy food changes your mood. I'm not referring to the Happy Meal box in some fast-food restaurants, although they temporarily change your mood. Red tomatoes, orange clementines, yellow lemons, green kale, blueberries, and purple grapes are some foods that will impact your body, mood, and chakras—the energy centers of the body I will review in a later chapter. If you enjoy those foods, the improvement will be instantly noticeable.

3. **Nature.** Spending fifteen minutes in nature is enough to remove dense energy in your body. Thirty minutes will refuel a nice level of good energy, and forty-five minutes will give you extra gas until the next nature encounter. Anyone in the service or healthcare industry with extensive contact with people needs at least forty-five minutes in deep nature every week—at a minimum. Nature is the organic energy-recharging medicine available to us for free. The altruistic trees, grass, and flowers are so happy to see and connect with us because we have a symbiotic relationship with them. They take the carbon monoxide we breathe out and transform it into oxygen. That's how they nurture themselves and us. Plus,

our energy rises when we're around the color green automatically.

4. **The Sun.** Spending ten-fifteen minutes in the sun, even if only at a window from indoors during the winter months, can drastically increase your energy. Try letting the sunlight hit your stomach and heart area. Take in the warmth, and experience your energy increase instantly.

5. **Early Meditation.** Spending five minutes early in the morning for meditation can do wonders for your energy and health. The first moment you wake up is the most influential moment of your day. If you start with positive energy levels before you're seduced by low energy from around you or worries from the day, you'll be better able to maintain positive energy throughout the day. When you wake up, you're refreshed, and your energy is naturally high. Meditation helps you keep it that way longer.

6. **Sleep.** When you sleep, you take a break from your habitual negative thought processes and reset your mind. Ideally, as you start to wake up, hold on to positive thoughts and concentrate for at least five minutes before getting up. It works! As you wake up, start thinking positive general statements such as "I love my life," "All is well," and "I love the easy flow of my life." Stay "general" and away from the

big issues you may be dealing with because they can bring your energy down until you can master your emotions.

There are major benefits to 30-, 60-, and 90-minute naps. For instance, you can reset whatever mood you're in. Naps often give your body the additional opportunity to heal ailments. Also, a 90-minute nap may get you in the Alpha and Theta meditative states where most deep personality changes can occur.

If you had a fight with someone, take a nap. If you are stressed at work, take a nap.

7. **Exercise.** Walking, cycling, playing soccer, dancing—any physical activity—will improve your energy if you enjoy it. And if you love the exercise, it will have an immediate impact—noticeable enough for you to want to do it more often. Walking on the beach will give you a double energy lift because you're exercising and near water in nature. Bicycling on a green trail is also a double energy lifter.

The point is to choose at least one of these suggestions and make it part of your daily and weekly routine. Start by doing things you enjoy—for example, eating strawberries in the morning if you like strawberries. The color red will energize your root chakra, which oversees your ability to provide self-care with food, shelter, security, etc. Maybe you already walk regularly, but now, you'll do it during lunchtime or drive to the park at the end of your day. You can mix any of the suggestions during the week. Remember, you must enjoy the activity!

Note. People not used to being in nature may strongly react to the idea of taking a thirty-minute walk outside. I'm not suggesting camping in the woods atop a mountain for a week (unless you want to). Because being with nature is the most natural way to lift your energy, try it—even if you don't want to. I have noticed that people who haven't been in nature for a while tend to not want to go for a walk. But once they're there and have a leisurely stroll with no hills or rocks, they revive their natural connection with nature and feel the difference in their energy.

What will you do today to shift your energy?

Chapter Five

HAPPINESS CHANGES NAMES

The second night, sleeping beside my mother, went pretty much like the night before. I gave her medication as late as possible so I could sleep uninterrupted a bit longer—just as I had given my babies a bottle as soon as possible to hopefully sleep more soundly.

The next morning, I returned to my mother's house to continue donating furniture, selecting things to save, and giving items to my brothers and those in need. The original mission had changed from getting rid of everything to getting rid of *almost* everything. In the drawers, I found papers from 1985, receipts from the supermarket and the pharmacy, telephone bills, prescriptions from 1988, X-rays from 1999, credit card and bank statements, electric bills, and old Christmas cards. It was like her past lived in the present, waiting to be rescued.

I felt a strong compassion when I recognized her vision and strength had been worse than we realized. Could it be that her cataracts saved her from seeing her home's dust collection and chaos? Which one came first—the cataracts or the dirt?

I still felt overwhelmed and moved from one side to another without completing one area. Clutter does that to people. I found old and brand-new things still in boxes—never opened. The house's energy was so dense that even for someone like me, who knows how to work with energy, it was difficult to concentrate on the task.

As I boxed things to go and answered a call to negotiate with the buyer to buy the closet and the broken coffee table, I found a carbon copy of a letter my mother had written to her sister, who lived in Salvador. She saved a carbon copy of every letter she wrote. My mother used to type her letters on a manual Remington typewriter even though she had beautiful handwriting. My father purchased the typewriter for his business, but we used it to type school papers in high school, and my mother still had it.

I started to read her letter, and by the end of the second paragraph, I called out to my brother, who was in the second bedroom packing. I read the letter out loud from the beginning, and my tears soon became uncontrollable.

The letter was dated September 26, 1984. It was a response to her sister's letter. I don't have my aunt's original letter, but it's easy to make up the letter she must have written to my mother.

I won't transcribe the four-page letter, but it responded to my aunt's accusation that my mother had

taken money from her mother after Grandma sold one
of her houses. My aunt wanted some money my grandmother had sent my mother. My mother told her sister
that Grandma called her in tears one day because my
aunt had mandated that she receive a part of the money
my grandmother earned after selling one of the houses
she built with her sweat money. My mother didn't know
of their agreement and told my grandmother that she
was still alive and didn't have to give money to any of
her children.

My grandmother knew of our family's financial situation and sent my mother money from the house sale.
My aunt claimed that the money belonged to her, even
though my aunt didn't help with the building of the
house.

My mother also told her sister of the difficulties our
family had endured, how we lost two apartments for
lack of payment, how she went back to work in 1983
to support the family, and how she paid two years of
late school tuition because my father wasn't making
any money. My mother told her that the financial help
my grandmother gave us wasn't coerced and that she
accepted the money because, many days, we didn't have
money to buy food.

In the letter, my mother shared gratitude to her sister
for helping their parents during the final days of my
grandfather's life. Mom reminded her that she would

have done the same had she lived nearby. Mom couldn't even go to her father's funeral because we didn't have the money for her to travel.

The saddest part of the letter was my mother's views of her life's difficulties. "It was my punishment from God for running away from home at age twenty-nine to be with my husband." Her parents had not approved of the relationship.

With the reading of the letter and the tears it brought to my eyes, the fifth wisdom arrived:

**"We have the right and the responsibility
to find our own happiness."**

CONNECTING WITH THE DESIRES OF THE SOUL

Who runs away from home at age twenty-nine? It's well beyond the right moment to begin a life and find your own happiness. It's the right of the soul! Often, we look in the rearview mirror and think that some of our choices were wrong, and sadness and resentment build. The truth is that our deepest desires push us to act in search of happiness, even if the path doesn't look happy from the perspective of others. Everything we do is because we think it will bring happiness or avoid pain. Right, wrong, or indifferent, the action is what we can do at that time according to the circumstances of the moment and our level of consciousness.

If a mother yells at her child, it's because she doesn't have the ability to do something different at that moment. She indeed has a choice to speak calmly and explain her point, but at that moment, it isn't possible. Perhaps a headache, work frustration, an unconscious reaction, fear, or ego leads her to raise her voice. It's all a consequence of the level of connection with her soul.

If my mother decided to leave her parents' home, work, family, and friends to be with the man she loved, that was what she wanted at the time based on her heart's desires and her level of consciousness. It was her choice to make.

We all have a choice based on our connection level with our souls. We create anger, sadness, and resentment when that connection is weak. When the connection is strong, we engage in conversation and make our points calmly, clearly, and consistently. Others can scream, but we stay centered and hold our space without the influence of lower energy levels. Nevertheless, there's no reason to beat ourselves up for not having a higher level of consciousness fifteen minutes ago or seventeen years ago when you yelled at the child or left your home.

Imagine that you own a Ferris wheel with a remote control. You don't have to wait in line or hire an operator because it's yours. You wake up one morning to find that the wheel has stopped and is waiting for you to embark. You get on, and it starts moving fast, just the way you like it. Of course, if anyone tries to jump on while it's spinning fast, they won't be able to get on. If they try, they'll be pushed back.

The same thing happens with our connection to our soul. When we get up in the morning and meditate or pray before checking the phone, email, or the news, we can easily connect with our souls. The connection is slow but firm at first, and with thoughts of gratitude, positive thinking, love, and a good healthy meal, the connection gets stronger and faster, like a Ferris wheel. Bad news, negative people, and negative energy cannot enter our space. They're repelled. We're almost invisible to those energies because they're at a different vibration. That's how we make choices that support our deepest desires and how life begins to move with ease and flow.

Things that happen to us are not good or bad from the soul's perspective nor punishment from God. God never punishes—EVER! God loves. These things we name "good" or "bad" are situations we create consciously or unconsciously. They exist without definition because we don't completely understand or know the soul's plans and are often unaware of our deepest feelings and thoughts.

Yes, we inadvertently create the accident, the eviction, the loss of a job, the lack of money, the sickness, the divorce, and the fights. We have the right to reach for our happiness with the freedom that God, a higher source, universe—whatever you want to call it—gave us. He doesn't interfere in our conscious or unconscious selections. It isn't that God was watching my mother be run over by a car and let her be hurt. He knows she has the right to create her life and soul's desires. This is why we have impulses that even we don't understand.

When bad things happen, we still have one more choice: to accept or not accept it. When we accept what is, we reconnect with our soul and find happiness within the journey. When we reject what is, we prolong the pain, accident, or job loss.

There are no mistakes in our choices when we reach for our own happiness. There is an infinite wisdom at work, conspiring to help us be happy. Every day, we discover new things, and our desires change. Short or long, we can make the road to happiness easier or harder. It's still the road to happiness, which is up to us.

What are the desires of your soul? Some people reach out to psychics, tarot readers, Buzios (a divination using cowrie shells), professional counselors, God, angels, priests, Pai de Santo (male priest of Afro- Brazilian religions), and so on for answers. But only you can know the desires of your soul. I don't condemn getting guidance from these sources, and some of them may be just what you need to hear to get on your path to happiness. All these may lower the noise around you that is stopping you from hearing it from within, but in the end, you are the one who can connect and decide what you want to be, do, or have to be happy. Your soul wants you to be happy. It is up to you to discover what makes you happy.

AN EXERCISE FOR DISCOVERING YOUR SOUL'S DESIRES

Here is an exercise to help you "remember" your soul's desires. Yes, I did say "remember" because the soul knows everything from the beginning. This meditation can be downloaded at www.ana-barreto.com/meditations

SOUL-CONNECTION MEDITATION

Find a quiet place where you won't be interrupted for fifteen to twenty minutes, and sit in a comfortable chair.

1. Rub the palms of your hands together for five to seven seconds. Take three long, deep breaths through your nose and exhale through your mouth.

2. Gently close your eyes and imagine a bright white light circulating over your head.

3. Then, imagine the light going into your head, traveling down your body, going through your brain, and removing any thoughts that no longer serve you.

4. The light moves down your eyes, removing any blockage from your vision, down your nose and mouth, removing any blockage to your voice, and

down your neck, removing any communication blockage.

5. The light reaches your heart and enters every artery, bringing light to every part of your body down your arms, hands, and fingers.

6. In your mind's eye, you can see how your chest gets brighter from the light in your heart, and you feel it, removing any heartache that no longer serves you. The light continues down to your stomach and belly button, removing any negative emotions that are holding you in the past.

7. The light travels down to the base of your spine and circulates around your sexual organs and hips. It then moves down your legs, feet, and toes, exiting through an imaginary hole at the tip of your toes.

8. Now, bring your attention to your heart, and imagine a small bright light in the center of your heart that's the size of a penny. This light is growing and growing, lighting your heart and spreading throughout your entire body. You can feel the warmth of the light in your body.

9. The light now comes out of your body through the top of your head and presents itself in front of you. This is a divine light. This light is your soul.

10. Feel the love that your soul feels for you. Feel the infinite love. Feel the unbelievable, enormous, unconditional love your soul has for you. Let tears come, and stay with the love coming toward you and going from you back to your soul.

11. Ask your soul, "What's my calling in life?" Wait to hear an answer. Ask a few times until you hear, feel, and know the answer. The answer may come like a quiet voice, a thought, a knowing, a picture, or a feeling. Trust that knowing, and don't second-guess it. You might not fully understand the answer yet, but let that be OK.

12. When you've heard the answer, open your eyes and write the message down. Then, close your eyes again and stay with the feeling for a few minutes.

13. In your mind's eye, see your soul returning to your body through the top of your head, down through your neck, and returning to rest in your heart.

14. Touch your heart gently, and thank your soul for the presence and wisdom that has been shared with you. Open your eyes again, and write any additional notes that come to mind. Know that you can contact your soul at any moment. Your soul's love and wisdom are available to you whenever you request it.

CONVERSATION WITH YOUR SOUL

The experience of feeling unconditional love from your soul is immense and intense. The first time you contact your soul, it's very common to feel strong emotions (sadness, relief, excitement, happiness, etc.) as though you were returning home after years and years of a long journey away. Some feel like they have just dropped the world's weight, while others feel the extreme fatigue of carrying such a weight. Some feel a deep relaxation, combined with knowing that all is well.

The second time I did this exercise was exhilarating. The meeting with my soul was wonderful. That was the beginning of a strong feeling of self-love. Don't worry if you don't experience something exhilarating like I did or cannot release negative energies at first. Trust the wisdom of your soul. It will happen to you when the time is right.

Some people don't get to ask questions during their first encounter with their soul because their emotions are overwhelming. Again, don't worry; communication is open, and you can return anytime.

Others will doubt the message they get, thinking that it's just their imagination or their mind playing tricks on them. Know that a very small percentage of people will actually hear voices. Most people will have a strong thought pop into their head. Your emotions will confirm if this is your soul or your ego. When the ego has stepped in, you'll feel fear. Suddenly, you'll feel afraid that your soul will tell you that your calling is to not be in your current profession of twenty years. Breathe. Know that when your soul answers, you will feel a sense of peace like you already knew the answer. You may cry.

Pause now and try it if you have not done so yet.

After the fact, your mind may try to rationalize the event and create doubts because there's no way to "prove" the wisdom. Remember that when you work with your soul, you use your heart, not your mind. The more open you are to the process, the stronger your connection with your soul will be, and all your doubts will disappear.

A side note: Although it's possible to have this connection with your soul at any time of the day, the best time for this exercise is in the morning—immediately after you wake up. That's when your energy is most expansive. After you've been to work and run around from place to place, your energy is more likely to dissipate at night.

Once you establish a daily meditation practice and your Ferris wheel is running high, you can hear your soul anytime, even without doing the full meditation. All you will need then is to ask, and it will come to you. Try it!

And remember: The path to happiness has many trails. When you honor your soul's desires, you can't go wrong.

What are your soul's desires?

Chapter Six

PAY ATTENTION TO YOUR EXPERIENCES

My mother's washing machine sat quietly in the laundry area, waiting to be sold or stored in my brother's house. There was no dryer. In Brazil, the weather does the job better and cheaper.

My daughters don't know what it's like to wash clothes by hand. I'm not talking about the small lingerie or the delicate sweater that must be hand-washed. I'm talking about sheets, towels, tablecloths, heavy jeans, blankets—all the big stuff that had to be stroked against the washboard and squeezed by hand to the best of your strength so that it wouldn't take too long to dry in the sun.

As young as ten years old, I had to wash my clothes. Thank God it wasn't like cooking rice and beans—we didn't have to do it daily. At first, it started as a punishment for something I did, and then it became a regular chore, like setting the table, washing the dishes, sweeping the floor, or dusting the furniture.

If I could wash and squeeze my mother's letter, I would have rivers of sorrow, guilt, and shame still hanging on the clothing line to dry into a shrinking spirit after many years of self-abuse.

I also found a large pot in my mother's home stained from years of cooking beans that almost burned. Before the pressure cooker, that's how we cooked beans—on the stove, monitored by intuition and experience by the women of the house. You can never forget the smell of burned beans. There was the constant fear of burning them, and there were tricks to improve the taste if they did burn. Back then, we couldn't discard the beans because there were no other beans to cook or extra money to buy more.

I now understand why mistakes were highly consequential in my house growing up—from dropping the fork from the dining table, breaking the bathroom towel rack, and burning the food. Punishment was a theme for any deviation. Like food shopping, Saturday morning was the "reconciliation" day. Any child who misbehaved during the week had a meeting on Saturday mornings.

During the week, my father came home late and tired and wouldn't be bothered by his children's lack of common sense. Often, when we didn't sneak to bed before he arrived, he would give a heads-up about Saturday morning. All of us would go to bed early when we had done something to award a Saturday meeting. We were naïve and hoped that our father wouldn't find out or perhaps forget a Monday or Tuesday issue by the time Saturday came around, but he usually remembered. Trying to do better on Wednesday, Thursday, or Friday didn't make it any better. In the end, we behaved extra well in the later days and suffered in silence for the entire week in anticipation.

Some weeks, it brought six to twelve hand slaps with a heavy wood brush designed to brush my dad's suits. In other weeks, the punishment was being forced to kneel on the hardwood floor, holding the arms straight sideways in the hallway for what felt like hours, and being humiliated when the apartment's front door was open, and our friends would see us there. Having to tell our friends what we had done added to the punishment. Other times were belt slaps, but those were more in the moment when we did something wrong on Sundays or holidays.

My mother wouldn't interfere unless my dad was beyond severe, only with extreme caution. Otherwise, she would get into trouble, too. Sometimes, I resented my mother for not protecting me from the physical abuse, even though she would console me afterward. Today, I know those actions taught me to protect my girls like a bear.

There were a few non-punishment days in our house: Christmas, Good Friday, Easter, and birthdays, even though I did get hit on my birthday once for lying. I hadn't even lied that day. My father was sleepy when

I asked him for permission to lend the volleyball to a neighbor, so he forgot about it and thought I had lied and lent the ball without permission.

When we became adults, my siblings and I confronted my father about those Saturday mornings, and he denied ever punishing his children. "Punishments were what I endured as a child," he said. "You all don't know what punishment is." I guess each generation improves a bit.

My mother tolerated my father's secrets through the years, yelling, verbal attacks, harsh treatment, and multiple suspicious affairs. She made sense of all by assuming that it was her punishment from God for running away from home at age twenty-nine.

The truth is that without those difficulties, my mother would never have found the courage to confront her husband and go back to work, restart her career at forty-eight years old, secure social benefits, have credit, open a bank account, and become an independent woman (until the day of her accident).

It was through reflecting on my childhood and my mother's life that I understood the sixth wisdom:

"The difficulties in life are not God's punishment but our soul's attempt to direct us towards our path."

God didn't punish my mother. She, herself, did it *unknowingly and severely.*

Her soul gave her small signs and pushes, and when she didn't recognize those signs, it gave her a big push to go back to work and secure her financial independence, which she had desired for years. The days with no food or unpaid bills were small signs from her soul to take control of her own destiny.

Anything that makes us slow down or stop is a nudge from the soul. It's like having an invisible bodyguard always watching out —but only if we choose to pay attention.

The calls from the soul don't have to come in big pushes that send you to your knees in a crisis, such as home eviction, job loss, a car accident, a serious illness, or an unexpected divorce. Often, the calls come like a little message—a friend's suggestion that pushes your buttons, an article in the newspaper, a passage in a book you can't put down, the occasional headache that doesn't go away, a repeated dream, a radio interview that upsets you, the occasional insomnia. All are messages from the soul; if we have a poor connection with our soul, we ignore those messages.

Rage, resentment, anger, depression, addictions, over-work, and overscheduling are common choices (conscious or unconscious) that stop or reduce the connection we need to maintain with our soul or spirit. We don't have to live in a church, temple, or mosque to make a connection with our soul (unless we want to). All we need is to make time to connect with our soul, hear its voice inside us, and follow its impulses. The longer we wait to pay attention to the soul's call, the stronger the nudges become. My mother called these nudges "difficulties." What do you call them?

PAY ATTENTION TO ENERGY
WHAT IS YOUR LIFE TRYING TO TELL YOU?

So, stop today. Take a deep breath. Look at your life. Look at the great things happening. Appreciate them. Look at the difficulties. What is your life trying to tell you? Really, don't rush through this. Pause it and reflect: Based on what is happening in your life right now, what is life trying to communicate? Is it a whisper or a scream?

We often hear the nudges of our souls and don't have the courage to follow through on what we know we must do. If this is the case, strengthen your connection with your soul, and *courage* will arrive on the schedule.

God is a mother—abundant in wisdom. God waits, helps, motivates (through others), and inspires but doesn't interfere. Imagine a mother teaching a child to walk. She holds the child's hands and walks from side to side, practicing until the child is almost ready to take two or three steps alone. Then, she lets go of the child's hands. The child falls after a few steps, and the mother starts the walking practice again. Sometimes, the mother buys a baby walker to help the child feel more secure, and eventually, the child starts walking independently. Other times, the child is still afraid of falling and takes a bit longer to walk, but the mother doesn't think her child will never walk. God operates in similar ways. God knows our potential and lets us fall, so we learn how to get up and walk again. But it's our choice. We all have immense potential for creating what we want, but first, we need to know what we want on a conscious level.

God didn't make my mother go back to work sooner or stay with my father. It was her choice when she was ready to do it. God doesn't make us do anything we don't want to do. All God wants is for us to be happy.

The uncomfortable feelings that difficulties bring help us to discover what we want, and they can, if we allow it, propel us into positive action. If we continue to complain and blame others, though, our difficulties stay back longer than necessary.

PAY ATTENTION TO ENERGY

During the day, our energy changes in intensity. When we sleep, our energy is high. When we wake up, our energy is still strong and tranquil (if we had a good night's sleep). Then, when we get up, the change starts. With negative news, our energy constricts. With the smile of a baby, the arrival of good news, or the blooming of flowers outside the window, our energy expands.

These things that we experience aren't "good" or "bad" unless we label them as such. Our opinion about our experiences is what changes our energy.

For example, if I'm stuck in a traffic jam, like the ones in Rio, and get annoyed that I'll be late for work, my energy constricts. But if I'm sitting in the same traffic and hear an interview on the radio that gives me an idea for improving something at work, my energy expands. The traffic is the same, no matter what.

We have the choice to expand our energy all day long based on how we view the events of the day. This isn't easy, of course, but it's possible. It's a matter of focus and practice.

The majority of our reactions to events, people, and things are automatic, requiring no thinking on the part of the mind. Naturally, by the time we have conscious thoughts about something, we have already had a knee-jerk emotional reaction. This isn't a negative thing most of the time. After all, if we had to stop and think about how to react to everything, life would be too slow.

Studies have shown that we think thirty-five thousand thoughts a day, but 95 percent of them are the same thoughts we thought the day before, last week, last month, and last year. If we think the same thoughts over and over, it isn't so hard to change our thoughts. We can start with one at a time. Any thought that causes our energy to contract, we can work on by changing it to a thought that causes our energy to expand. Then, we practice that thought until it becomes a regular positive reaction to events. The key is to pay attention and reprogram our automatic reactions to things, people, and events. It starts with what you focus on.

REPROGRAM THOUGHTS THAT DON'T SERVE YOU

The first step is to identify the emotion you're feeling—bring it to a conscious level. Then, search for the thought that has caused the emotion. Once you find the thought, change it to a better thought that will give you a more peaceful emotion, and continue to practice the new thought until it becomes a habit.

The next time an incident triggers a negative reaction, you'll be able to more easily derail the reaction and change it.

Get a pen and notebook, and write down answers to the following questions. (You may want to revisit it at a later time to practice, practice, and practice.)

1. What reaction or emotion do you frequently have that doesn't serve who you are, who you want to be, or where you want to go? Is it anger, fear, frustration, insecurity, or negativity?

2. When was the last time this happened?

3. What were the thoughts you had about the event, person, or thing that caused the emotional reaction?

Be mindful that sadness and anger come so quickly that it can be difficult to pinpoint the cause. Just stay with the feeling and keep thinking about your opinions about the person, thing, or event.

4. Are those thoughts absolutely true beyond a reasonable doubt?

5. What are other positive thoughts that you could have about the event, people, or thing?

6. How would you feel if you changed your thoughts about the event, people, or thing?

7. What emotional reaction would you have to the new thought?

Here is how I used this exercise in my life:

When I got home at night after a long workday, I would frequently feel furious about finding a mountain of dirty dishes in the kitchen sink and on the counter that I had left cleaned and organized in the morning. I would yell at my daughters and make them clean it immediately. Often, I'd be so upset that it would ruin the rest of my evening. My daughters, meanwhile, would get upset, too, and feel that I was overreacting. In my mind, it was a reasonable request: Clean up after yourself!

Here's how I answered the seven questions with regard to that situation:

1. What reaction or emotion do you frequently have that doesn't serve who you are, who you want to be, or where you want to go? Is it anger, frustration, insecurity, or negativity?

   Answer: *I feel anger over the dirty dishes in the sink when I get home.*

2. When was the last time this happened? Bring the emotions to mind.

   Answer: *It happened two days ago.*

3. What were the thoughts you had about the event, person, or thing that caused the emotional reaction?

   Answer: *My children don't appreciate me and take me for granted. I'm a full provider for them, and they don't appreciate my efforts. My life makes their lives happen. They're taking advantage of me. (At that moment, I cried because I hadn't verbalized the thought until then.) Washing the dishes is a reasonable request.*

4. Are those thoughts absolutely true beyond a reasonable doubt?

   Answer: *It took me a while, but the answer was no. I am not 100 percent sure that my children don't appreciate me.*

5. What are other positive thoughts that you could have about the event, people, or thing?

Answer: *My children forget to wash the dishes. People forget things. They plan to do it later and get distracted. The kitchen is not that important to them. They're not making a mess to hurt or upset me. They just forget.*

6. How would you feel if you changed your thoughts about the event, people, or thing?

    Answer: *I would feel calmer and more relaxed. I'd be able to enjoy my evening even if I found dirty dishes in the sink.*

7. What emotional reaction would you have to the new thought?

    Answer: *I would calmly ask them to wash the dishes. And if I couldn't wait until they were ready, I would wash the dishes myself. Washing the dishes would not kill me.*

PAY ATTENTION TO YOUR EXPERIENCES

Now that you've identified the thoughts causing the negative emotions influencing your life experiences, it's time to hear the voice of your experiences.

Find a quiet place like a park bench, deserted beach, or garden to sit for a while. Ideally, you want to be in nature. Get a brand-new notebook and a brand-new pen or pencil. This will tell the universe that you're ready for a new beginning. You may want to get a warm cup of your favorite tea, a blanket, a throw or scarf, or anything else that brings you comfort. Yes, you can drink coffee.

Take a few minutes to connect with the space. Notice the beauty of the place: the sky, the grass, the birds, and the trees. Make it a point to list the beautiful things you see.

Then, write down your answers to the following questions. Remember, there are no wrong answers. The more you write, the more you'll connect with your unconscious thoughts. Make sure you leave plenty of space between the answers, as you'll go back to review them later and may want to add more notes about what you discovered during the process.

1. Think back, and list all the difficulties that keep repeating in your life. Odds are you have one main theme happening already. Maybe it's the reason you bought this book.

2. When did the difficulty start? How old were you? Where did you live? Who did you live with? Take time to write your answers, and don't discount anything that comes to mind.

3. If you were creating those difficulties, what possible reasons would you have for creating them? List all possibilities, even if they seem unreal. Don't rationalize.

4. Now, list any judgments you have about each of the reasons (real or unreal) in your answers to question #3.

5. Read the reasons and judgments, and select the one reason that feels more likely to be true.

6. What negative feeling or thought do you have that is causing this difficulty?

7. Is this absolutely true?

8. On a new page in your notebook, reverse the feeling into a positive statement, and write the positive statement down nine times.

9. Read the statement every morning, afternoon, and evening before bed for your subconscious mind to assimilate it into your life.

Here's an example of how this exercise can work:

1. Think back and list all the difficulties that keep repeating in your life.

    Answer: *I can't keep a job for more than three to five months. I quit or get fired.*

2. When did the difficulty start? How old were you? Where did you live? Who did you live with?

    Answer: *It started when I went to work for company X. I was twenty-five years old and lived with my boyfriend.*

3. If you were creating those difficulties, what possible reasons would you have for creating them? List all possibilities, even if they seem unreal. Don't rationalize.

   Answer: *I don't want to work. I don't like to work. I want to win the lottery and be rich. I want to be self-employed.*

4. Now, list any judgments you have about each of the reasons (real or unreal) in your answers to question #3.

   Answer:
   I don't want to work—people who don't work are lazy.
   I don't like to work—there's something wrong with people who don't like to work. They have no ambition.
   I want to win the lottery and be rich—I'm more likely to be struck by lightning than win the lottery.
   I want to be self-employed—I can't earn a full salary being self-employed.
   There are no great jobs for me because I don't have a college degree—I'm stupid because I don't have a college degree.
   I can count on my parents to pay my bills—only losers rely on their parents at age thirty.
   I want a man to support me—husbands must support their wives.
   I don't want to be out of the house all day—I can't find a part-time job that pays my bills.

5. Read the reasons and judgments, and select one reason that feels more likely to be true.

    Answer: *There are no great jobs for me because I don't have a college degree.*

6. What negative feeling or thought do you have that is causing this difficulty?

    Answer: *I feel shame, and I feel inferior because I don't have a college degree or a career at age thirty.*

7. Is this absolutely true?

    Answer: *No, many people without college degrees have great jobs and full careers.*

8. On a new page in your notebook, reverse the feeling into a positive statement, and write the positive statement nine times.

    Answer: *Statement: I feel confident I can find the ideal job for me with the help of my soul.*

9. Read the statement every morning, afternoon, and evening before bed for your subconscious mind to assimilate it into your life, even if you don't believe it yet. Stick to it, and in time, your subconscious will accept it as true.

Imagine how it would feel to have the right job that matches your talents. See in your mind how you would walk if you had the right job. Would your posture be different? How would you feel? What words would you use to tell people what you do for a living? Feel the positive emotions, and release any negative thoughts that may try to creep in.

Know that your soul will guide you to the right path at the right time. When you feel anxiety or frustration, focus on how you will feel when you work at a great place using your talents.

Note. When you write your new statement or affirmation, your subconscious mind will tell you it isn't true. Practice ignoring that voice because it isn't your soul talking. With practice, your mind will "change its mind," and you'll attract opportunities to show evidence of your professional talents.

Remember. The voice of the soul doesn't judge, criticize, complain, or put you down. The voice of the soul helps, motivates, guides, and understands. The voice of the soul is serene and calm and fills you with a feeling of peace and love.

"Trust your soul."

How do you punish yourself? Could you stop it? How can you improve your energy?

CHAPTER SEVEN

THE PRACTICE OF SELF-COMPASSION

Another working day went by with more packed boxes, piles of donations, and trash. At the end of the day, I took more of my mother's personal belongings and my mother's letter to my sister's apartment. I let my sister read it. Then, I reread it several times, each time understanding aspects of it even more. It was clear that my mother took the high road by understanding and forgiving her sister's offenses and accusations. She knew that my aunt didn't know all the details and events that had happened between my mother and grandmother.

I'm sure my mother didn't intend for anyone else to read her letter outside her sister. In my family, it was an unspoken rule never to ask questions, especially about the past. The few stories I had heard from my parents were examples of how privileged we were compared to their lives as kids.

I learned my mother's life story during a time of "besabafo"—the outflow of words and emotions held inside—a few days before my wedding day when I asked Mom why she had married my father. I had wondered that all my life. My mother was a beautiful woman—

thin, composed, and proper. My dad was overweight, unattractive, and aggressive, although he was a good dresser and most likely a great lover.

My fiancé paid for my parents' air ticket from Brazil to come to our wedding in 1992 because they didn't have any money. We went shopping for my mother's dress at Macy's for her to wear at the wedding, and at lunch, she told me that she met my father outside work one day. She didn't like him at first, but he was persistent. He would wait for her daily, and they would ride the bus together even though he lived in the opposite direction. He would walk my mother to her street but not the front door because my mother didn't want her parents to know about him yet. She said my father was a smooth talker.

One day, she arrived home after my father left her at the corner of her street, and her father was waiting for her outside the front door. My grandfather told my mother that my father's wife had come over to their house and told them about my father's marriage and four children. "You're forbidden to ever see him again!" my grandfather told her.

My mother had no idea my father was married, so she felt emotionally destroyed.

The next day, my father was waiting for her again outside of her job, and she walked faster, trying to avoid him. She told him that his wife and two of his children had visited her parents. He told my mother that he wasn't married and that the woman wasn't his wife. He said that the woman was his mother's housekeeper. She had thrown herself at him, and he got her pregnant. She wanted to marry him. With that story, my dad convinced my mother that he wasn't married, and the two of them went to talk to her parents.

My grandfather didn't buy my father's story and again forbade my mother to see him. Sometime later, she ran away from home to be with my father.

My mother made it a point to tell me that she didn't have sex with my dad until they moved in together. In Brazilian terms, they were "somewhat" married since he put a roof over her head in 1963. They talked about getting married, but it wasn't until after she was pregnant with my older brother that she found out the truth. My father had lied, as he was married. So, my parents never got married because my father never got a divorce. I later learned that it was true that the woman who visited my grandparents lived with my father's mother. It was also true that he had gotten her pregnant, but he had been forced by his mother to marry the woman. He was in his early twenties, and he didn't take the marriage seriously because he was dating my mother.

At my dad's funeral in 1997, I met three of my half-siblings for the first time. As I walked into the cemetery, I saw a younger man who was the spitting image of my dad. Apparently, he looked at me and thought the same thing about my appearance. Dad's legal wife was there, crying over the coffin, like she was the "wife," while my mother stayed silent at a distance.

A few days after my dad's funeral, my siblings and I were going through his papers, and we found the birth certificate of my youngest half-sister. She was twenty days younger than my older brother.

My mother also told me that a few years after she ran away with my dad, she learned that her father became very ill after she left. My mother was his favorite daughter, and my mother's departure broke his heart.

My mother's mother, Maria, was very strict with her daughters. She would lock the door at 10:00 p.m., and my grandfather would unlock one of the windows for my mother and her sisters. My mother would cook his favorite meal and iron his clothes just the way he liked. She would also give him a heads-up if my grandmother was "on the wrong side of the stove" on any particular day.

My mother's biggest regret was being unable to attend her father's funeral. She didn't have any money to take the bus home nor anyone to look after her six children. The day she learned of her father's death, a telegram arrived in the morning. Around noon, when we would set the table for lunch, my mother pulled the white table runner off the dining room table and broke a large vase full of white gladiolus flowers. She ran into her bedroom and closed the door. I didn't know it then, but that was the image of guilt.

As I've said, twenty-one years after the rebellious act of leaving home at age twenty-nine, against her parents' wishes, my mother still saw her life problems as a punishment from God that she felt she deserved. One of the greatest things about my mother is that she always forgave everyone, including my father, for the things he did. She rarely has bad things to say about people, and when we complain, she used to say, "Deixa prá lá," which means "let it go." She always had great compassion for others, but what about herself?

Reflecting on these experiences of my mother, I understood the seventh wisdom:

"The best expression of compassion is self-compassion. It's when we open our hearts and feel self-love first before sharing it with others."

WHAT IS COMPASSION?

Compassion is the act of feeling empathy when others are hurt and, to some degree, sharing their pain. Compassion isn't the same as pity or patting someone on the back. Compassion is love that's expressed.

Why are so many women able to feel compassion for others but not for themselves? I'm certain that if my mother went to a bookstore and selected a book to read that told her own life story, she would feel huge amounts of compassion for the protagonist. We work, and we take care of our children, partners, friends, and relatives. We cook, clean, do laundry, drive children to social and sports activities, take care of medical issues for everyone, including aging parents, and support the school, the church, and the community. But at the end of the day, we don't give ourselves the time and respect to regain the energy we gave out freely. We give everyone a break but not ourselves. This is a lack of self-compassion.

The history of women giving to others before themselves has roots in early ages. It seems that we continue to self-punish ourselves for the "sins of Eve." Eve's story, fact or fiction, opened the door for women to question the status quo.

I believe that Eve wasn't a sinner for eating the forbidden apple but a heroine! She dared to eat it and, with that, brought to light the way people (men and women) think about women and the expectations of them.

Unconsciously, we continue to contribute to the group consciousness of our female ancestors that women are "less than," "the lesser sex," or "the last one in line" when we're actually responsible for bringing the next generation to greatness. How can we do great things for others when we don't do great things for ourselves?

We need to make the time to care for ourselves *first*. And it is not selfishness; it's self-love. We silently blame our parents, our spouses, and our children for our lack of time for self-care, but the responsibility lies with us. Happily, I see improvement in the views of women in our culture today. However, there are still too many of us hindering the progress of other women because we teach our daughters to not have self-compassion. Even though we may tell them otherwise, they learn from our own poor examples.

When we don't care about how we feel, how much we do, or how much we have, we teach our daughters (by osmosis) to not love themselves, and we teach our sons that this is okay. We could tell our daughters to take care of themselves, but they learn from what we do. This is why it takes many generations for change to happen. The habits are ingrained in us unless we make a rigorous and conscious effort to change them.

Self-love is the first love we feel. Then, we learn to love our parents, our brothers and sisters, our friends, our children, and our partners. As we age, we forget our innate ability to love ourselves because we assimilate the behavior of the adults around us, either as we watch our mothers being treated or as we are being treated by others.

We give others much more of a break than we ever give ourselves, but that can change. It needs to change.

HOW TO AWAKEN YOUR SELF-COMPASSION

The last time I asked a friend about self-compassion, she shared that she had plenty. And then, she worked two weeks straight without a day off until she got really sick when she could have asked for help and said "no" to babysitting her grandchildren. We don't know if we have it until we are tested with actions.

Here is an exercise to improve your self-compassion. When you get up in the morning, before taking a shower, look at your naked body in the mirror for five minutes and observe your thoughts. I know you don't want to do this but stay with me. Any aversion reaction to do it is an indication that I may be right, and many women struggle with self-compassion. Try it. It would be beneficial for you to see what comes up for you. Usually, the negative thoughts come fast, especially if you're accustomed to criticizing yourself regularly. This will give you an idea of how you mistreat yourself.

If you love every part of your body, are grateful for every inch of it, and celebrate your existence, congratulations! You're a small percentage of the population.

If you're like most people and notice the fat on your legs, the wrinkles on your face, and the scars on your belly, take note. Please don't use your thoughts as yet another excuse to beat yourself up. Just take note of the thoughts without further judgments. After you take your shower, write down three to five critical thoughts you had about your body.

If you have about five of those thoughts in five minutes, and you have about thirty-five thousand thoughts a day, then these negative thoughts represent about seventy-two hundred "lack of self-compassion" thoughts a day. Adding the fact that we think ninety-five percent of the thoughts from the day before, by the end of the week, these thoughts add up to about forty-seven thousand thoughts in which we put ourselves down—every single week—unconsciously.

It wouldn't be nice if every time we passed by a mirror, we would compliment ourselves with phrases such as: "Hello Beautiful; You look amazing today?"

I learned that force of will alone is not enough to move the needle from lack of self-compassion to full self-love because we're starting from such a disadvantaged point. We need to transform and transmute the negative thoughts.

UNCOVERING MORE SELF-COMPASSION

There is self-compassion and self-love that already exist in all of us. We can uncover it if we heal the hidden pain from our past. Most of it we felt in childhood from conception to seven years old. The incidents during those years created who we are and may still have a hold on us as adults. From early childhood, we heard negative messages from our parents, teachers, relatives, and friends. We were scolded, punished, criticized, or not encouraged. By the time children start talking, they have already assimilated the negative thoughts and behaviors from the people around them—by the truckload. They learn what behaviors will be rewarded or punished. Please don't blame them. They don't know any other way.

My daughter Erica's first words were "Mom," "Da," and "no" by the age of six months. By her first birthday, she had her indicator finger up to tell other kids, "No, no, no." Guess where she learned that from? You guessed it. I was her teacher.

There are two types of thoughts: thoughts of love and thoughts of fear. The thoughts that evoke the word "no" are thoughts of fear, even if they were initiated with loving intentions. Thoughts of love are thoughts that evoke the word "yes." When my child wandered near the ungated stairs, my first reaction was to say "no" instead of calling her attention to a toy away from the stairs. My fear of her falling was transmitted in three ways (body, mind, and spirit), even though my loving intention for her safety created my negative reaction, which she assimilated early on.

My grandparents' fears that led them to forbid my parents' romance in 1963 started many years before that day in Salvador. Perhaps it came from my grandfather's abandonment by his father at a young age, which made him think he had to protect his daughters. It's quite normal to want to protect your child from falling down the stairs or from having her heart broken, but everyone, even babies, has the right to create their own experiences.

In Brazil, before the active use of bleach, white clothes faded slowly over time, and stains weren't removed with one of those stain removal pens that we carry in our purses these days. To deep clean the clothes or remove stains, my mother would wash the clothes with detergent and let them soak in the sun for a few hours before rinsing them with water. That's what we call "quarar" in Brazil. Not too long ago, I tried it on some of my grandmother's hand-embroidered linens from the 1930s that had yellow stains from aging when the cleaner didn't want to touch them. It still works!

We will do a similar process to remove the thoughts of fear and let true love and compassion emerge in our lives. We will bring those unwanted thoughts to the light. Note that I did say "emerge" instead of "build" or "grow." That's because there's an infinite amount of love and compassion already inside of us, and all we need to do is delete the fear clutter that doesn't serve us anymore.

The process is simple. First, find the emotion that is creating the fear. Feel it in your body. See if you can recall the age when the fear began to develop. What event happened at that age that might have initiated the thought? You don't need to know what thought it is yet, just the event. Once you find the event, look at the conclusions you made about the event at the time. Clear the thought by bringing it to the light of consciousness and let it soak there for a while. Then, rinse it by acknowledging that you no longer need that pattern of thought and release it.

Here's an example: Let's say when you were five years old, your parents had a terrible fight. They yelled at each other, and you heard them. You felt afraid. As you dig deeper, you realize that you concluded at such a young age that you were at fault for their argument and that if you were a good girl, they wouldn't fight anymore. So, you decided that you would always be a good girl, and things wouldn't be so scary anymore. Perhaps you are still avoiding confrontation and don't speak up for yourself based on that experience.

GETTING RID OF FEAR

Each time you have a negative emotion, ask yourself:

1. Where do I feel it in my body?
2. Look at the chart on page 152, find the area of your body, and determine at what age you learned that fear.

3. Read the energy center (also called chakra) information corresponding to the age when the issue developed.

4. Recall any events that happened at that age. Trust your intuition. If you struggle to remember, ask your parents and relatives to help, if possible. Notice discomfort in your body; it will help you remember the emotion. If this is a big issue, your protective ego will try to stop you from remembering, so you may have to try a few times. Most big emotional issues are spun from traumatic life events, such as death, birth, divorce, loss, illness, and so on.

5. Once you remember the event, bring it to consciousness by asking yourself, "What conclusions did I make about this event? What did I decide was true as a result of this event—about myself, others, or the world?" Don't brush off these conclusions as infantile. The conclusions may make no logical sense to you as an adult, but what happens is that these conclusions stay hidden in your unconscious mind and still drive your behavior. Because the habits were created so young, however, we aren't aware that illogical beliefs are driving our behavior.

6. Imagine that you remove the emotion and the thought from your body and place them in a bal-

loon. Tie the balloon and imagine it flying out into the sky and out of sight into the universe.

7. Say out loud, "With this, I let go of this energy that no longer serves me so that it can be transmuted and transformed. I give thanks for this lesson."

This is a simple process, but it can only work if you're willing to feel the temporary discomfort in your body and face your fear. When you're ready, your soul or spirit will guide you to transmute and transform the fears because love is your natural state.

I did this exercise with a coworker who felt terrible anxiety and anger every time she needed to do something new or encountered something undesirable. Her reactions didn't match her usual behavior at work. She was highly competent and had a fair share of successes under her belt. But when her anxiety was activated, she wouldn't sleep for days in anticipation of the new event or upset. She wouldn't eat either. I asked her why, and she did not know. She shared that she felt a pain above her belly, below her breast. I told her the location of the pain represented a time when she was three years old. (See the Chakras of the Body explanation that follows.) I asked what happened when she was three, and she said, "Nothing. My parents were great." Finally, after I continued to question her, she said, "The only thing that happened when I was three years old is that my sister was born. I don't remember, but my parents told me that I had a hard time with the attention she was getting from my parents. She's such a pain, and we don't get along. She was younger, and she was always competing for my parents' attention."

"Could it be that you felt you had to always do better to get recognition from others, perhaps putting more pressure on yourself than you needed to?" I asked. She gave me a shy smile and started to tell me about growing up with her sister and parents. Her anxiety at work had nothing to do with the new tasks but with her fear of not getting the "recognition" she needed from others. Her ego projected her upsetting reaction when she was at risk of not being the best.

Once she brought the actual issue to consciousness, released the old thoughts and feelings to be transmuted, and felt compassion for her younger self, who concluded that she was less than the new baby, her anxiety, sleeplessness, and starvation decreased. These traumas have many layers, and it takes time to dissolve them, but they can be extinguished.

THE CHAKRAS OF THE BODY

It is important to know where you feel the fear in your body and then find the corresponding chakra and the age when the fear developed.

There are seven main chakras of the body and two small chakras in the palms of our hands. The chakras are energy centers in the body. We all have them, and they have even been photographed. They're responsible for our well-being, emotional development, and our connection with the physical and spiritual worlds.

All seven chakras are fully developed by our first seven birthdays. During each year, a chakra governing an area of our life flourishes and helps us become who we are meant to be in this lifetime.

Here is an overview of each chakra:

Base Chakra— The first chakra develops from conception to age one. This is the energy center responsible for our basic needs of shelter, food, safety, and security. The base chakra is located at the base of the spine for men and between the ovaries in women. When we're fed, changed, held, and cared for by our parents at that age, we feel safe and secure. If we're neglected during this time, we'll tend to feel insecure about safety and money. We also pick up on our mothers' emotions during the pregnancy. Her concerns about money, food, and shelter (real or unreal) can also cause us to feel insecure.

Spleen Chakra— The second chakra develops from age one to two. This is the energy center responsible for creativity (creating energy) and sexual energy, also called the "lower heart" in women. The spleen chakra is located two inches below our belly button. When life goes well, a child is allowed to explore, and the parents provide and maintain a mostly uneventful daily life; the child is able to create dreams, manage addictions, and maintain healthy relationships. When the child has inconsistency and/or trauma during this time of development, blockages can occur. People with blockages may develop addictions, poor relationships, and sexual dysfunction. This center works together with the fifth chakra, the heart center. Artists create from this energy center. Highly creative people with blockages in the fifth chakra will submerge in the second chakra energy and have periods of high creativity and no love, or they'll have periods of high sexual energy and no creation.

Solar Plexus—The third chakra develops between ages two and three. This energy center is responsible for willpower and is located below the chest and above the belly button. If this year in a child's life is uneventful, they will have strong self-esteem strong self-control, be able to deal with authority well, and act on intuition or gut feeling. When strong trauma occurs during this time, a child will have a hard time taking responsibility for their life, will learn to manipulate others, or will tend to be manipulated.

Heart Chakra— The fourth chakra develops between ages three and four. This energy center is responsible for the ability to give and receive love, compassion, and affection. A well-nurtured child will be able to express love and also give, receive, and feel emotions. When a child is neglected and experiences any trauma during this time, they will have difficulty being in a loving relationship, be highly judgmental of others and self, and have difficulty loving and accepting self. A woman with blockages in this chakra will default to using the lower heart (second chakra) for love by working her sexuality.

Throat Chakra—The fifth chakra develops between ages four and five. This energy center located in the throat area is responsible for the ability to communicate and show up in the world. During the development of this chakra, children who are allowed to be themselves with no major criticisms are able to show themselves to the world just the way they are and communicate well. Children with critical parents will struggle to advocate for themselves and be who they want to be.

Third-Eye Chakra—The sixth chakra develops between ages five and six. This energy center is responsible for our mind's eye. It is our knowing and where we have access to the wisdom of the ages. This chakra is fully open in children. As they grow and are dismissed, reprimanded, and criticized for their thoughts, feelings, and imagination, the center becomes blocked so that they have little to no access to the wisdom there. Children allowed to express their thoughts, feelings, and imagination will grow up to trust their intuition and create a world beyond their time. This center is also connected to the second chakra. Possibilities are quickly originated here and then created in the second chakra.

Crown Chakra—The seventh chakra develops between ages six and seven. This energy center is responsible for our connection with the Divine. Through this center, located eight inches above the head, we find the energy connection with God, a higher source, and spiritual beings. This is where we receive divine guidance. Children who are severely punished and threatened with hell and other mystic beings will fear this connection with the spirit and close it. Children who are taught that God is love will be open to exploring a close spiritual connection.

Hand Chakras—There are two small chakras located in the palms of the hands. These two small but powerful chakras are developed between the ages of four and five. They have healing energy power that develops simultaneously with the heart chakra. They're responsible for our ability to heal people, give love, and bless our homes, water, and others. We are all healers. People who have chosen the path to heal others have cleared any blocks that exist in their path so that they can fully use the energy of these chakras.

The picture of the 7 major chakras, the 2 small chakras, and the ages when they develop is below.

The Seven Major Chakras

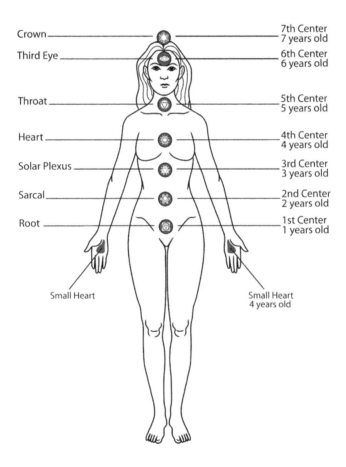

Crown — 7th Center / 7 years old
Third Eye — 6th Center / 6 years old
Throat — 5th Center / 5 years old
Heart — 4th Center / 4 years old
Solar Plexus — 3rd Center / 3 years old
Sarcal — 2nd Center / 2 years old
Root — 1st Center / 1 years old
Small Heart — Small Heart / 4 years old

Everyone's chakras go in and out of balance throughout life. Any blockages developed in childhood or adulthood can be unblocked so that we can reach our highest desired potential.

By practicing the Getting Rid of Fear exercise on page 144, you will learn to recognize the thoughts of fear by noticing the feelings in your body. These thoughts don't feel good. It may seem like a long, arduous process when you consider your thirty-five thousand thoughts a day, but it isn't. As I've said, these thoughts are very repetitive. Plus, you can work on only one or two thoughts at a time.

It's easier than you think when you pay attention to your feelings and the sensations in your body. If you have any bad feelings, find out what thoughts caused it. When we learn to catch these thoughts and correct them with love, we can diminish the self-criticism in a matter of days. Self-compassion is very powerful! In a few weeks, you'll notice that you begin to say "no" to actions that no longer honor your desire for self-compassion and say "yes" to activities that enlighten your spirit. In a few months, you'll find yourself acting more loving toward yourself and your life going the way you want it to flow.

OBSERVING HOW YOU TREAT YOURSELF

When we start the journey of self-discovery, we notice how much we mistreat ourselves. You may be thinking now, "I don't think I mistreat myself." The truth is, we all do it to some degree. When we work through lunch and pull over at the fast-food restaurant to eat in the car, we mistreat ourselves. When we stay late at work to finish a project due in a few days instead of going to yoga class or staying up late baking muffins for a fundraising event instead of going to bed and getting a good night's sleep, we mistreat ourselves. When we volunteer on our day off when our laundry is two piles high, and folding is done at midnight, we are mistreating ourselves to a degree. There's nothing wrong with helping others, but begin to notice when you overdo it at the cost of your well-being. If there's an imbalance between how much you give others compared to how much you give yourself, it's time to look at how you are treating yourself.

How do you treat yourself?

Everyone needs a dose of self-compassion from time to time, and many people need it daily. This is a process of self-discovery, and it can be a bit painful in the beginning but also liberating. The freedom you feel from releasing the blocks of pain you have caused yourself (most of the time unconsciously) will make you wonder how you managed to live that way for so long.

Remember, it isn't necessary to blame anyone or to blame circumstances. A part of the process is to take full responsibility for where you are today and where you want to be on the path of self-love and self-compassion.

When I learned and practiced this process, I noticed how much I had been criticizing myself and others in my head. I never told the people what I thought, and I didn't realize how much I was hurting myself. Being negative is exhausting! When I began to correct these thoughts (and one never stops correcting their thoughts), my life started moving in the direction of my dreams. I felt centered daily and learned to care for myself before caring for others. I began to give myself the same number of breaks that I gave other people. I learned to give myself more love. This translated to action when I learned to leave work earlier, get a manicure or reflexology, tell my daughters to walk to school so I could sleep in, tell my friends "no," and even schedule naps on my days off.

Many people may find it selfish. However, selfishness is not being able to share with others. When you practice self-compassion, you learn to share what you have without hurting yourself. The more your own pitcher is filled and overflows, the more you'll have to give others, and you'll end up giving from a place of power instead of a space of depletion. When you're whole, your giving is full, lengthy, and self-reproducing.

SELF-CARE AND THE UNIVERSE

One of the hardest actions for women is to care for themselves before their children. I'm not saying that you let your baby cry in the middle of the night because you need sleep. However, you do need to sleep during the day when the baby is sleeping before you do the laundry, cook for the family, go to the supermarket, or clean the bathroom. One of the most amazing things you'll discover when you practice self-compassion is that when you decide, consciously and guilt-free, to let the kitchen be messy so that you can take a nap, you'll wake up feeling rested, centered, and together. Suddenly, cleaning the kitchen is an effortless task because you aren't exhausted. Plus, self-care is energizing.

I found that volunteers frequently showed up to help with the laundry and groceries because the universe supported me in supporting myself; deadlines got extended, traffic jams cleared, meetings got canceled, snow days showed up, etc. Over and over, I have witnessed that the universe gives me more when I love myself first.

IMPROPER GENEROSITY

Improper generosity is the same as lack of self-compassion. It's giving what we don't have. It seems like a cliché, but we've all heard on the airplane before takeoff that we need to place the oxygen mask on ourselves before helping others—even our baby. It's common sense. If you faint because of a lack of oxygen, you can't help anyone. You would die, and so would your baby.

At times, the excess of improper generosity seems small, like drops falling in a bucket. In time, however, the bucket becomes full and will overflow. When you've given too much to others and not enough to yourself, other important areas of your life don't receive the attention they need from you. That's when you begin to encounter health issues, pay fees late, lose a home or job, deal with relationship issues, or miss the last train because you're overextended.

Don't get me wrong — I'm not against generosity. For years, I received great generosity from many people, and I'm generous when I'm called to be. Recent research has found that the person who helps others receives more benefits than the person who receives the help. The benefits are mental, physical, and biological. In the study, the people who were generous were found to have an increased sharpness of their mental ability, were healthier than before, and produced more endorphins, dopamine, and serotonin—the hormones responsible for health and vitality. They actually measured these in the laboratory!

The question is, do you need to help others or not? Of course—help others. But take care of yourself with self-compassion first. Check-in with yourself to make sure that the help you offer comes from a full heart and not from a sense of obligation or a feeling that you aren't worthy unless you help.

THERE'S NO SUCH THING AS A MISTAKE

Another area where women are a little less compassionate with themselves is when they feel they have made a mistake. Actually, mistakes don't exist. What we call mistakes are actions and decisions that we make based on our level of consciousness at that moment. Life has many paths and side roads. We can do everything except live backward (unless you're Benjamin Button).

There are no mistakes, only choices that provide opportunities for us to learn. If mistakes existed, then we could go back to the past and correct the errors. Then, I would go back in time about three days and eat only one "brigadeiro" – a Brazilian chocolate truffle that is so easy to make- instead of a whole plate that gave me a stomachache. (Okay, but that's just my example.) But what we call mistakes are simply lessons in life's journey – Don't eat a plate full of brigadeiro.

When we see a baby trying to catch a wasp and the baby gets stung, we don't say, "What a stupid child!" In reality, we feel compassion for the child, understanding that she has learned a hard lesson.

Many times, your choices don't make sense to others. People looking in from the outside say, "She must be crazy!" But those people don't know the agreements you have with your soul. They don't know your heart's inspiration or the call from your spirit. Your choices only turn into mistakes when you judge them as such or allow others to do so.

No one deserves to suffer, but we suffer when we compare our lives against something or someone's idea of what it must be. The judgments of others turn into our own prejudices. Eventually, we feel that our lessons —what people call mistakes—make us less deserving of our own compassion, and we sometimes even feel that we have to over-give to others in order to justify our existence.

There is no need to justify your existence. You are as deserving as anyone else and should not be judged by anyone.

Self-compassion extinguishes the self-judgment that calls life's lessons "mistakes."

Find the recipe for the brigadeiro—Brazilian chocolate truffle—at the end of the book.

What area of your life could you infuse a dose of self-compassion?

CHAPTER EIGHT

THE BODY, MIND, AND SPIRIT OF AFFIRMATIONS

On day six, I woke up earlier than the previous days but stayed in bed, meditating and unsuccessfully trying to stop thinking about my mother's new life. Ten months prior to her accident, she received a registered letter stating that the house she had rented for years was going to be demolished for the World Cup and the Olympic Games. My sister and brothers took the opportunity to look for a better location for our mother to live closer to my sister, who has the flexibility to assist my mother with doctor's appointments and the expertise in maneuvering the medical system.

I knew that the eviction letter woke up the dormant giant of all punishments within my mother. At that time, Brazil was a major player in world events, and that anticipation caused real-estate prices and rent to soar. When Mom couldn't find an affordable place to live, the giant was poked ferociously.

During that sixth day, I saw the quiet desperation in her face as she prayed with the rosary. She seemed to be pleading with God. *She doesn't know she's a divine soul*, I thought. Perhaps the difficulties of the years were intended to remind her to look for joy; instead, as happens with so many of us, her problems made her forget to look at all.

My mother calls her six children "my inheritance—the only 'possessions' my husband left me." Her feeling of security is her children. Her retirement income is not enough to cover all her bills because she spent many years not working in order to obey her husband.

My mother grew up poor. My grandmother took in the wash but had no running water in the house. My mother and her sisters picked up the loads and walked to the stream to wash the rich people's clothes by hand. The clothes were then squeezed and brought to dry in the yard. Finally, they were ironed with a heavy manual iron that was heated on the stove.

My grandmother also put herself through culinary school as an adult, ensured her daughters went to school and built two houses during a time when women couldn't own houses without a husband's or father's permission. She supported the family while her husband, who worked as a truck driver, spent a good part of the money going to dances.

At that time, women also couldn't have a bank account without their husband's signature. Actually, they could open it but not take money out without a man handling the transaction. My grandmother pushed her children to study and get a career, but only my mother and her older sister got through school. My mother earned a technical degree in accounting, and she worked as an accountant's assistant for a few years before she met my father and left that job to run away with him. My mother grew up in a consciousness of lack, hard work, obedience, and fear of God.

Before the accident, when my mother felt pressured by my siblings to go and live with one of them, she would call me in New York to get my support against them. I would listen, agree with her, and then call one of my brothers or sister to remind them that she had not been given the right to choose for most of her life. I tried to convince them to back off and let her live alone for as long as she wanted and could.

"Our mother went from her parent's house to her husband's house where everything was chosen for her—everything from the brown church dresses to the living-room curtains she hated. She deserves to make her own decisions," I would say. Now, with her injury, it's like she's back in prison. She said to me many times, "I can take care of myself! I don't want to live with your sister or brother!" And look where she ended up.

On those calls, I could hear the worry and anxiety in her voice about finding a place to live. I agreed to send her more money so she could widen the house search.

About a month or so before the accident, she found a house without a kitchen in a bad area, but my siblings didn't allow her to take it. I agreed with that. She was willing to go down many notches to have a place to live without her children.

A week before the accident, my sister had found a one-bedroom apartment near her house that was perfect for my mother. In Brazil, renters are required to have a cosigner who guarantees payment in case the rent isn't paid, and the cosigner must be a homeowner. Earlier, my sister recalled how happy and relieved my mother was on the morning they signed the contract, knowing that she wouldn't have to live with her children. Later that day, the accident happened.

That morning, between meditating and remembering the events prior to the accident, I understood the eighth wisdom:

"We can't fight against anything because fighting leads us toward the very thing we don't want."

THE LAW OF ATTRACTION

Perhaps if my mother had gone along with receiving support from one of her children, the accident wouldn't happened. It is the law of attraction—like attracts like. My mother was fighting against living with her children and being dependent on them. For the past few years since my father's death, this was the only thing she fought about. Today, she's living with her daughter and is more dependent on her children than ever before. It would have been better to focus on "living by herself" instead of "not living with the children." These are too different intentions.

The universal mind can't distinguish between "to live with the children" and "*not* to live with the children." The universe only hears "live with the children." We need to focus our full energy—body, mind, and spirit—on what we *want* rather than what we want to *avoid*.

Everyone says, "Think positive," and we believe the thought, "Don't be dependent," is positive, but notice the word "don't." That makes it a negative statement. The positive form of the statement would be, "I am independent"—present tense and what we want, not what we don't want.

Here's another problem my mother had: her beliefs about the high rent in her area. If you don't believe you can afford the rent, you're likely to create that very situation. A lower rent will show up, and you can't see it. Her panic during the house search and her constant complaining about the high prices, as well as her insistence that she didn't want to live with my siblings, all created an energy within her that attracted what she didn't want.

Here are more examples of how to turn our affirmations positive so that we're more likely to attract what we want:

Negative	Positive
I don't want to be poor.	I am prosperous.
I don't want struggles.	My life is harmonious.
I don't want problems.	I am content.
I don't want a divorce.	I have a happy marriage.
I don't want to live with my kids.	I live independently.

Have you tried using the law of attraction without any luck? I understand the Law of Attraction as 50 percent knowing and 50 percent believing. The main reason the Law of Attraction doesn't work for some people is that they change their minds before giving enough time to come to fruition.

Another phenomenon that has an impact on the Law of Attraction is "desperation." The more desperate we are to be, have, or do something, the less chance we have of attaining it. Desperation is the fear that what we want might not be possible to achieve. Remember that there are mainly two energies: love and fear. Fear doesn't bring abundance, happiness, or harmony. Desperation is the emotion of fear.

After my mother's first surgery, when she was in the hospital, one of her friends called to tell her that she had heard of a vacated house. "The house isn't great, but you can 'make do' with it," Mom's friend said. The house was in an area where gunshots were fired almost weekly. Incredibly, my mother wanted to secure that house and even asked her friend to place a deposit. This is what desperation does.

To manifest what we want, we need to feel as though we already have it. The *feeling* of having it is key. But if you settle for less, like my mother, it's the same as telling your subconscious mind and the universe that you changed your mind and no longer want a nice house in a safe neighborhood.

BELIEFS IN THE WAY OF OUR DREAMS

Just like my mother didn't believe that she could find an affordable place to live, your own beliefs could be in the way of your attracting what you want. If you desire to be rich, but you believe that rich people are corrupt and greedy, abundance will continue to elude you. If you believe, like my mother, that you deserve to be punished for the things you did in the past, happiness will never arrive. Or if it does, you won't recognize it. If you believe men are liars or always adulterous, those are the types of men who will show up at your door. When a great guy asks you out, you'll turn him down because you won't be attracted to him—and you won't know why.

The saddest part of all is that when we attract these things based on our beliefs, they only substantiate our beliefs. We say, "See! I knew it!" It's confirmation. It requires some work on our parts to counteract our beliefs and what *appears* to be confirmation of those beliefs.

It doesn't matter how many positive affirmations you say if you have an underlying belief, that's the opposite. However, taking a lot of time with positive affirmations can often help you to replace negative beliefs with positive ones, as long as there is no desperation.

So rather than second-guess your desires or blame the universe for what isn't working in your life, ask yourself a few questions, such as

"Why did I ask for this situation in my life that I don't want?"

Yes, you unconsciously asked for it. It's hard to accept, and it's no reason to beat yourself up because we've all done it! But the faster you acknowledge what's really taking place, the faster you can change your beliefs and create what you truly want.

THE WAY TO CREATE AFFIRMATIONS

The reason you write affirmations is to make sure the universe and your subconscious mind are absolutely clear about what you want. They also help you face any doubts you have about your desires.

In continuing to work with the feng shui principles in your life, the following will help you focus on a few areas of your life and help you reach your desires.

There are nine main areas of life. In the Bagua that follows, you will see these areas: Career, Helpful People or Travel, Creativity, Relationship, Fame or Recognition, Finance, Family, Knowledge or Spirituality, and Health. I strongly suggest that you select only three of these areas that need your immediate attention and write affirmations (intentions) for them to keep your energy focused. Later, you can write other affirmations.

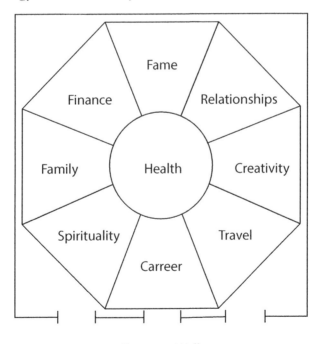

Entrance Wall

Important. As you get ready to write your affirmations, remember that we all create our lives daily by the thoughts we think, the words we use, and the emotions we feel. As a result, most of what we create is done unconsciously and unintentionally. So, pay attention to what you say, think, feel, and do that may not be in line with your affirmations.

Creation is a three-level process: body, mind, and spirit. You can write all the affirmations you want about creating a relationship (body—physical manifestation). Still, if you think (mind) that there are no good guys around where you live and don't imagine or visualize (spirit) the wonderful dates that you can have, you'll only be working on one level and may not be successful.

Here is a full example: Joanne can't find a job. She gets up early every day to look for job listings online and sends two to three resumes daily. She has been out of work for four months, and her unemployment benefits are about to run out. Since day one of her search, Joanne has talked with her friends and family about how hard it is to find a job. Every email she receives turning her down puts her in a bad mood. When people ask her how she's doing, she responds, "Not good."

She writes the following affirmation: I *want* a great job earning *a lot* of money and being *stress-free*, where my boss is *not bossy*, and my *coworkers aren't lazy*.

Can you tell what's wrong with this affirmation? She can affirm it a million times a day, and she may get a job, but not a job where she'll be happy. She's violating the body, mind, and spirit rule of affirmations. Let us examine it in detail:

1. **Body.** She uses the word "want," which means she's affirming "wanting." If you "want" something, you don't *have* it. "A lot" of money is not specific. "Stress-free" is negative because there's no reason to bring up stress in the first place. "Not bossy" and "aren't lazy" are clearly negatives.

Here's an effective way to write her affirmation:

I enjoy working as a government employee, earning $80,000 or more a year. I have a great boss and coworkers and lots of room for promotion.

Change "want," "wish," or "hope" to "have" or "are." Instead of stress-free, use perhaps a "healthy environment."

Don't use affirmations to influence the behavior of others. You can't change others, only yourself. "My boss gives me lots of raises" isn't as strong as "My job provides me with the abundance I deserve."

If you struggle to believe your affirmation is possible, you can change it to something more general that you can accept until you expand what you believe is possible for you. For example, "Every day, the universe organizes to bring me the work I desire."

2. **Mind.** Joanne thinks about her old job all the time and talks about how poorly they treated her. She already has poor expectations of the jobs she applies for and anticipates that she won't get them. In fact, Joanne doesn't even think she's qualified for them. If you want a new job but keep thinking about the problems you experienced in your current or previous job, you send conflicting messages to your subconscious mind and the universe. It's like complaining about rice and beans every day even though you keep eating them. Remember, we think the same thoughts day in and day out. It's up to you to change those thoughts if they don't serve you.

Be certain of what job you want! Too many people change their minds. You can certainly change your mind, but your affirmation needs to match your choice. Then, try not to flip-flop.

3. **Spirit.** Joanne feels bad every time she gets a rejection email. She feels sorry for herself and blames her old boss.

Be mindful of judgments you have about your desires. If you don't think it's possible, change your judgments or generalize the affirmation. Take a day or two to write your affirmations. Use the affirmation meditation that follows if you have difficulty discovering or deciding what you want. Often, fear creeps in, and we settle for the familiar and secure (my old job) instead of the heart's true desires.

When we work with affirmations, we must imagine what feelings we will have when the affirmation becomes reality. If you want a new job, imagine yourself feeling the excitement of going to work on the first day. What clothes will you wear? Imagine the happiness of meeting new people and receiving the first paycheck or even going on vacation with the money you make. How does all that make you feel?

The mind from the previous step—your thoughts— will set the feelings in motion, so these three steps are interconnected. Your subconscious mind doesn't know what's real and what isn't. Your thoughts are just as real to it as something you hold in your hand. So imagine the situation you want as often as possible, and allow yourself to really feel the emotions of having it.

This part of the process is very important. Top athletes practice this technique daily by visualizing what it will feel like when they cross the finish line and walk onto the podium to receive the gold medal. Ice skaters visualize themselves making jumps perfectly over and over. Expect it to happen. Your true expectations will trump the desperation of not having it yet.

MEDITATION FOR AFFIRMATION

If you aren't sure what you want, don't beat yourself up. It's a common issue. This is because we don't make the time to be with ourselves. If you are like most people, you've been told that you *should* know what to be or do by now. And those side comments are not helping. The good news is that if you're dissatisfied with where you are now, you're well on your way because knowing what you *don't* want helps you know what you *do* want.

This meditation will help you become clearer about your deepest desires, release negative emotions about your desires, bring habitual thinking to the surface, and write your affirmations correctly.

CLARITY MEDITATION

Set aside 20–30 minutes for this meditation, but I suggest you do it on a day when you can relax. Some people may need 2–3 hours to recover from the emotional discharge that the meditation can cause. You will be releasing chunks of negative energy, so it's a good idea to take a long shower afterward and get a good night's sleep that evening. Make sure your phone is turned off and that you won't be disturbed.

Get paper and a pen, and find a comfortable and quiet place to sit. You may play relaxing music to help you connect with your soul. You can download the guided meditation on my website, www.ana-barreto.com/meditations. Read through the entire meditation, even if you download it from the website. Select one area of your life from the nine areas of the Bagua on page 169. Always work with one area at a time and no more than three. Here are the steps of the meditation:

1. Close your eyes, take in three deep breaths through your nose, and breathe out through your mouth.

2. Relax your scalp.

3. Relax your forehead, eyes, jaw, and face.

4. Relax your neck and shoulders. Further, relax the tension in your shoulders. Busy people carry a great deal of energy in this area.

5. Keep breathing in and out.

6. Relax your upper back and lower back.

7. Relax your arms, hands, and fingers.

8. Relax your belly and hips. Mothers tend to hold more tension in these areas, so let go even more.

9. Keep breathing in and out.

10. Relax your legs, feet, and toes.

11. Now, imagine a bright-lavender, healing, and relaxing light circulating about nine inches above your head.

12. Imagine this light penetrating the top of your head like a light breeze, removing any remaining tension in the area of your head, neck, and shoulders.

13. The light keeps moving down, releasing any unnecessary energy in your heart, belly, arms, and legs, exiting through your toes.

14. Allow the light to go down into the earth, down to the center of the planet, until it reaches a very heavy anchor. Tie the light to this anchor until it's very secure. This is your connection with Mother Earth.

15. Feel the nurturing energy of the earth getting larger and larger and returning to you from the earth. Feel it moving into your feet, legs, belly, heart, neck, and head until it exits through the top of your head and into the sky.

16. Place your right hand on the front center of your neck. Think of the area you want to improve, and ask out loud once and twice silently: "What is my work? What do I want to do? What is the work of my soul?" Keep asking the questions silently until you hear an answer from your soul. Remember to breathe.

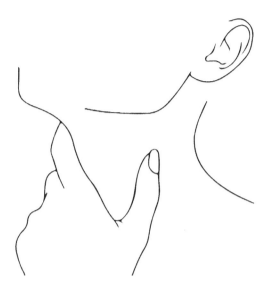

17. Gently open your eyes and write down the first thought that you receive. Don't worry about typos, and don't judge the thought. Keep writing every thought you have for a few minutes.

18. Next, close your eyes again and place your right hand on your neck. Ask out loud once and twice silently: "What negative thoughts do I have that are interfering with the desires of my soul?"

19. Open your eyes, and write the answers you receive. Ask the question as many times as needed until you feel you have the answer you're looking for.

20. Close your eyes, and place your right hand on the front center of your neck. Ask once out loud and two more times silently: "Where did I learn these negative thoughts?"

21. Open your eyes and write the answer you receive.

22. Close your eyes, place your right hand on the front center of your neck, and ask once out loud and twice silently: "What do I need to do to let the negative thoughts go?"

23. Open your eyes, and write the instructions of your soul.

24. Now, imagine a big balloon in front of your heart. Fill the balloon with all the negative thoughts you discovered today, all the negative learning from your past, and all the voices that have influenced you and no longer serve who you are and who you want to be. Imagine the energy leaving your body and entering the balloon. See the balloon floating up in the sky.

25. Say this out loud three times: "Today, I release these energies that no longer serve me so that they can be transformed by the universe. I thank you for the lessons, and I open my heart to love and wisdom."

26. Stay there until the balloon floats up past the Earth and the solar system, disappearing into space. Write down anything that comes to mind.

Now, it's time to write your affirmation. Revisit the instructions for writing affirmations to ensure that you meet the body, mind, and spirit guidelines.

Make a cup of tea and relax. Let tears fall if they come. Crying is a sign that you're connected to your soul. You may stay in silence or go for a walk outdoors. It's good to give your body, mind, and spirit an opportunity to work in unity.

The first time you do this meditation, you'll release large chunks of energy. You may cry or even feel a strong pain in the heart area. The more you cry, the more you'll release the pain. Your body will recover within eight to ten hours. If the pain is too strong, take at least thirty days before you return to do the exercise. That's a sign the healing has started, and there are a few levels of healing still to come. Be kind to yourself. Try not to work hard or take care of active children until the day after the meditation or at least that day. This is a very special time between you and your inner self.

Remember: It's okay to let things go! As you let go, you'll pave the way for acceptance and positivity. You'll be less likely to fight against what you don't want and focus on what you *do* want.

**What affirmation could you create today
to improve your life?**

179

Chapter Nine

STOP THE "BEARING"

Day seven arrived more calmly than the previous mornings. My mother still needed medication every so often through the night, but there was less preoccupation on my part. Breakfast was just like the day before, and so was bedding change. Before leaving in the morning to close my mother's house, I prepared a bean soup from the beans my sister had cooked earlier that week. My mother had to be on a special liquid and soft-food diet for at least another two to three weeks.

It took 14–18 hours to cook beans in the traditional way, as my mother and her mother have done before. They would sift through the beans to pull out any rocks, bugs, and spoiled beans. Then, the beans would be washed with lots of running water and soaked overnight to soften. In the morning, the beans would be checked again for rocks or bad beans that surfaced in the water and then washed once again. Mom would start cooking by 7:00 a.m. because the beans would take about three hours to cook on low heat. This was before we owned a pressure cooker.

Today, we freeze the beans in small containers and take much less time to cook them. (You can find my mother's recipe at the end of the book.)

When I was a child, cooking beans was a lesson in learning how to wait—just like learning how to wait for love. My mother would say, "Quem espera sempre alcança," which means "Those who wait always reach what they want."

Today, I know that there are two kinds of waiting: waiting with certainty and waiting with doubt. Waiting with expectation will lead you to reach your goal. Waiting with worry and doubt, on the other hand, will make you sick. Many women confuse waiting with "bearing" or tolerating the bad things in their lives.

BEARING LIFE

When I got to my mother's house, I found my wedding album among the papers and pictures stuffed in the closet. It made me remember how I didn't want to go to sleep the night of my wedding day because I didn't want my happiest day to end. It was more than twenty years after my wedding day, and I was happily divorced, still sorting through marital things. What should I do with the album? Perhaps I would give it to my youngest daughter since I still had another album stored in the "I don't know what to do with it" closet. Yes, even with my feng shui practice, I have a closet that has no purpose other than to store things I still can't discard. As I said earlier, feng shui is a process. You can't donate it (who wants someone's wedding photo album), and discarding it seems to be a waste of money. I can still save it for the girls. But then, maybe my daughters wouldn't want to be reminded of their parents' broken marriage and the pain it caused them.

Going through the album, I noted that my husband looked very handsome, and my father looked distinguished in a tuxedo. I couldn't believe the dress I picked for my stepdaughters. What was I thinking? My thoughts then went to the conversation I had with my mother in 2003 when I called to tell her I was separating from my husband. "How come?" she asked me. "I had a worse marriage than yours, and I was able to bear it."

I don't think this is what you want to hear from your mother when you tell her you're about to walk a dark, scary, painful, and uncertain path, especially when you've been avoiding it for years. For me, divorce was a major deviation from the road I'd been groomed to take all my life and the end of a long, happy dream.

I also recalled that I shared my fears of separating from my husband with my friend, Andrea, as well as the pain of having my soul mate try to make it impossible for me to go on my path to happiness. I still remember the little cuddly brown teddy bear Andrea sent me with a card that read, "Bear with it."

That day, as I packed the wedding album, I understood the ninth wisdom that my mother's life taught me:

"Bearing" our lives only fuels our fears and keeps our personal power dormant.

Even though it means to hold on, to support, or to remain firm, "to bear" is a destructive verb. It impairs our connection with our soul. Nothing beautiful or soul-connecting has ever involved the verb "to bear."

My mother has a PhD in "bearing," just like many other women. I was working on my own master's degree in "bearing" when I decided to drop out and get a divorce. Fearing for the finances, being discriminated against for being divorced, losing my home, and not affording a good life for my children were some of the reasons that led me to "bear" my marriage after it was over. Bearing was depleting my power as it does to everyone who exchanged their spirit for bearing unhappiness.

In 1988, my mother was bearing one of my father's indiscretions when he had an affair with my sister's friend, who was temporarily living in her house. She went on to "bear" a stroke just after she found out and didn't tell anyone. Bearing will physically damage your heart if you don't address it.

The few months before my mother's accident, she was "bearing" the stress of having to move and not knowing where to go. She was "bearing" the lack of availability of her children to go with her to find a home. She was "bearing" with the landlord, who didn't fix a roof leak for a few years. She was "bearing" with a coworker who pressured her to retire before she wanted to fully.

Somewhere in history, women decided that "to bear" was somehow honorable. We "bear" children! What is more honorable than that? Perhaps because of Joan of Arc and Jesus Christ, we took on the persona of martyrs. Women have become sympathizers. Perhaps the pain of childbirth influenced women to accept that bearing painful things in life is a good thing. Unconsciously, women have understood that "bearing" will purify the sins of women, which we never committed.

There's a big difference between tolerating abuse, disrespect, indifference, and being taken advantage of and accepting the consequences of a great cause because you have self-love, and there is a higher power calling you to it.

Humanity's goal is to be happy—always! God doesn't want us to be unhappy, no matter what religion has taught us. When we tolerate pain, we disconnect from our higher source. If "bearing" was acceptable, we would still enslave people, women wouldn't vote or be educated, and Jews would be living in concentration camps.

A WOMAN'S POWER

For eighteen years, I watched my mother "bear" bad things in her life because she felt she had to. She felt she had to "bear" verbal attacks, physical threats, and emotional contempt; She felt she had to "bear" watching her children be punished. She didn't see a way out of that situation. She had six children, no job, no money, and carried the emotional baggage full of guilt and shame that kept her stuck. As a child, I assumed my childhood was normal. It was all I knew because the other women went through similar conditions. As I became a teenager, I suspected it was not natural.

When I was twenty-six years old, my mother told me that she had wanted only three children but wasn't allowed to take birth control. After six children, she was able to reduce the bearing when her friend gave her birth control pills without my father's knowledge.

My mother felt she had so little power. I no longer blame my father, and I don't blame her either. They both were products of their time and culture. My mother had the choice, and she chose to bear, to pray, and to wait for a better time just as other women have done before her.

Many women learned to wait for tomorrow, which is a form of self-sabotage. Twenty-four hours indeed makes a huge difference in the way we think and feel. However, when we keep adding an additional twenty-four hours day after day to avoid dealing with issues that we know deep in our hearts must change, we are making a decision to procrastinate our happiness, even though we have not moved a muscle.

During times of frustration, Mom tried to compensate her bearing with advice to my sister and me: "Nunca dependa de homen," which means "Never depend on a man." That was her way to positively influence her daughters' future, which I was learning by osmosis. I tried to follow it passionately. I didn't want to lose my personal power. And I never wanted to bear the same trials as my mother, either.

But it turns out that I also gave away my power in the years of my marriage. There are many ways by which women lose their power. I lost mine when I didn't follow my heart and chose instead to please someone else to keep the peace, just like my mother did before me. I lost my power when I went against my own desires in order to make someone else happy by providing what I thought he wanted—even though he never told me what that was. It begins with a small thought that we must compromise. Each day, we begin to compromise just a bit more. After a while, you have over-compromised so much that you have lost yourself in the process. Women who don't recognize themselves in the mirror find ways to bear it. We are very resourceful that way. I would "bear" with it by being busy. I've met many women who "bear" by being paralyzed, drinking, and doing drugs. Having power is not about getting our way but about being truly happy. When compromising doesn't bring happiness, it becomes self-abuse.

How do you lose your power? Do you self-abuse? How do you avoid happiness? Do you get busy, paralyzed, or abuse drugs and alcohol?

I came to learn that too many women lose their power as early as age nine. We all have it when we're born. If you don't believe me, just look at the babies and how they can get you up in the middle of the night and have their needs met. Look at how happy they are and how much joy they spread around just by being present. That's the true nature of happiness.

When you lose your power, it's like when you misplace your cell phone. You know it's in the house, but you can't find it. You call the phone and realize you have it on mute. You retrace your steps and can swear you left it in the same place you always leave it, but it isn't there. You accept that you're going to be late and take a deep breath, only to find the phone in your purse or pocket. You had it with you the entire time.

The same is true of our power. We never *really* give our power away. We just lose sight of it. We keep it dormant and wait for something or some event to change. All we need to do is wake it up.

Many women confuse "to bear" with "to wait." We wait for the bus, we wait for the rice and beans to cook, and we wait for the water to warm up for our shower. But we need to stop tolerating physical, mental, and spiritual abuse. How long can one tolerate abuse for the sake of "bearing"? One day, two months or thirty years are all too long. These actions only take our personal power away. Without our personal power, we exist instead of living. Life was meant to be lived consciously.

THE POWER OF ACCEPTANCE

"To bear" also means "to hold onto." When we hold on too long to something that has served its purpose, we stop the flow of abundance, and I don't mean just money. It is also happiness, joy, prosperity, health, connection, and so on that lose the flow into your life. While it's hard to accept, loss is always good. Everything that goes makes room for something new to come. Sometimes, we miss the bus and later find out that it got into an accident. Other times, we lose a boyfriend who ends up being an unfaithful husband to his new wife. When we lose something, it's a sign of growth. We're ready for something better.

Instead of bearing or tolerating any undesired event, we need to learn to accept that what happens is for our well-being, even if it doesn't look like it. It's a mindset change. The beating, the abuse, the pain, and the loss of a loved one have happened for the greater good. We suffer because we want to change what it is. We can cry, be angry, be sad, mourn, and then accept it and move on at the appropriate time you need to accept it. There is a major power in accepting. It allows us to move forward. When we bear or tolerate what makes us unhappy, it weighs down the soul; with a heavy soul, you are no good for yourself or anyone else, as a matter of fact. People with heavy souls are depressed, spread negativity, experience anxiety, and contaminate the energy of every space and everyone around. When we learn to accept, we step into our power. It doesn't mean that we agree with what happened, but acceptance fuels the power you need to leap out of it.

What's the difference between accepting and tolerating? You can feel it in your body. When we accept, we use our personal power; we may be sad, but our emotions are centered, and we can easily go about our day and life. When we tolerate, we don't feel good, our power is being held hostage to our feelings, and we're tensed and stressed. We can't see abundance even if it stepped on our toes wearing a red-and-yellow polka-dot tutu carrying a purple elephant on its shoulders.

Fear is what causes us to settle on "bearing." The best medicine for curing fear is to face it and take action with love. When we drink water, it's because the body is thirsty. When we feel fear, it's because the soul wants to grow. Fear has its advantages when we are not paralyzed or distracted by it.

Let's build a new prospect about fear and faith so we don't avoid or become their victims. Fear and Faith are one and the same. They are not real. You can't touch either one. Fear shows up when we are called to grow. Faith is what we need to move past fear and leap into our brilliant life. They tend to show up in pairs. But if one of them crips in to stay, you have to choose faith.

The first step to growth is to have faith. When we have faith, we know that what we need or desire is on the way. When we take action, the fear is reduced. Doubts may arise along the way, but if we focus on what we desire instead of the fear and the reason we want it, fear becomes a catalyst and not a destroyer of our desires. Managed fears will lead you to take steps toward what you want instead of "bearing" your troubles.

Often, after taking steps, when we look back at our lives, we realize that fear kept us stuck longer than we needed to be. We discover that what seemed so difficult wasn't nearly as hard as we thought. You may think that you could have taken steps sooner, but this is faulty thinking. You didn't move earlier because you didn't have the level of consciousness you needed when you finally took action. You can only see it when you look back because you're wiser now.

You can follow your personal growth, which is a hint of fear. You can follow your safety and security, which fear will try to coerce you to follow by staying put, but you cannot follow both. Get to grow stronger, and safety and security will flow into your life naturally.

Accept where you are. No one takes action until ready. At the same time, don't spend your life allowing fear to dictate the "whens" and "hows" of what you do. When you finally decide to be happy, all the obstacles you see will be less important than your happiness.

We must let go of tolerating self-violation and accept the things that must go without anger or fear. When we know that everything that happens is for our own good, we move forward. There is a learning opportunity waiting to be discovered in each "bearing" of self-violation. The faster we accept the changes and move toward self-love, the faster our spirit grows, and the quality of our lives improves.

THE VOICE OF THE SOUL

It's important to learn to discern when we're fueling our fears. That's when we make time to connect with our souls. There are so many voices talking in our heads. We don't know how to distinguish which voice is the wisdom of the soul and which are the voices of fear. Note that I said "voices"—plural. Often, we hear our parents' voices, which is not always bad. Other times, it's the critical voice of a close friend or ex-lover. When we make time to hear the internal voice, the true voice will always be heard. All you need to do is to make quiet time and listen.

Remember, the voice of the soul is gentle, calm, and loving. It never judges, shames, or criticizes. It never uses the words "have to," "should," or "ought" because it knows you have the power of choice. It never causes anxiety. This voice evokes feelings of peace and truth. When we cultivate this relationship with the self, we access an enormous wisdom that has always been there.

The voice you hear is just like the voice when you count silently in your head from one to five. You know the next number. A regular daily meditation practice will get you there sooner. We make a connection with our soul by making time to hear its voice and letting go of the excuses that keep us holding on to "honorable misery," and we make room for moving in the direction of our dreams, desires, and happiness.

The other day, I had lunch with a close friend, and she shared some of the difficulties she had with her husband over the years. She shared verbal, mental, and physical abuse. She was still contemplating the time for her departure and said she had been living in survival mode for almost seventeen years. When we hear stories like this, our first thought is to judge, try to push her to act or be very sad for her. None of these actions will actually help her. She will continue on her path, and when she's ready, she will connect with her soul. It isn't easy to be in her shoes, we all agree. Only a strong connection with her soul will get her where she needs to be. Only she can do that for herself.

We women may tend to have strains of self-sacrifice genes in our DNA, but we also have strong personal power that can correct and heal any undesired strains in our DNA. It isn't the kind of power that fights, even though we certainly can, but it's even more powerful than that—it's the kind of power that creates and nurtures worlds—our world.

If you have to label any action you take as "self-sacrifice," it will not serve who you truly are and who you are becoming when you begin to do the inner work. If you are giving up your career to raise children because you want to be available for them and manage your home well, that's fantastic, and you are living in your power. But the moment you say or think that you are sacrificing your work potential to raise your children, you just disconnected from your power source. It is *not* what you do that will engage or disengage your power; it is what you think and feel about what you are choosing to do that *does*. The opposite also can be a disempowering action. If you are working and feel that you are sacrificing your family life to build your career, it is not powerful either.

Genes in our DNA can be changed, not only the expression of the gene. Science just proved it. It is important to be in your power—always or at least most of the time. You will make decisions that support who you truly are and who you are becoming. Plus, life will love you back. You will know that happiness is not something you work toward; happiness is living it now.

HOW TO CONNECT AND STRENGTHEN YOUR POWER

Find a green area in a yard or park. You can imagine if there is no grass near your location. Take off your shoes and feel the grass. Play with the grass with your toes, and close your eyes. Take three slow, deep breaths. Place three fingers over your gut—the space in the middle of your belly just a few inches below your breasts—and feel the energy of the area. In your mind's eyes, imagine a yellow light circulating around this area. Feel the emotions there, as this is where the energy of your personal power lives. Keep the light circulating, and imagine the light healing this area. Make room for your personal power to wake up. Feel the emotions. Ask your spirit to support you in this moment, and feel the healing.

Do this exercise as often as you like to help you strengthen your power. It's especially helpful if you're trying to build the courage to make a big change in your life. This is not a meditation that, when you do it, will give you the courage to immediately quit a job you have been contemplating or end a marriage that has been unhappy for years, although it might. This short meditation is a building block to fully collect your power from wherever you might have dropped it. Take back your power, and give up the belief that you have "to bear" struggles to be happy later. The power is yours. It always has been.

What "bearings" are you ready to let go?

Chapter Ten

WELCOME HOME TO ME!

On the day of my departure to New York, I woke up at 6:00 a.m., gave my mother her medication, and returned to bed. I got up at about 8:00 a.m., gave her the yogurt, and went to prepare her breakfast of oatmeal and *café com leite*. I changed her diaper, put her on a portable potty, gave her another wet-sponge bath, moisturized her body with lotion, dressed her, cleaned her surgery wounds, and changed the bandage, knowing that it would be a while before I could take care of her again. I brushed her hair, helped her into the wheelchair, and took her to the living room after she prayed with the rosary.

I changed the sheets on my mother's bed and gave my sister the task of doing what she does best—laundry. I also showed my sister how to make two more soups—cauliflower soup and beet soup—which would last another week. (The recipes are at the end of the book.)

As I began to pack my suitcase, my mother sat in the living room with the same distant air of sadness and disbelief as she had on day one of my visit. Still, I was happy with the progress we had made since the accident. Mom's house was closed, and her new room was cleaned, organized, and feng shui'd for health and prosperity. She would be recovering in her new living arrangements with my sister.

On the other hand, my heart was heavy, and my body was exhausted, not from all the work of the past days but from the weight of my thoughts about leaving my mother "unfinished." I knew, of course, that she was indeed whole. She only needed more time to process the changes in her life. Most of all, she needed to find her own wholeness.

Even though I missed my family when in New York, visiting them in Brazil had always been difficult. I can't say that it was ever really a vacation—something I'm sure a lot of people can relate to. Running from one relative's house to the next is not fun when you have a short week to rest. In the beginning, I did it out of family obligation. My family needed to meet my children. I needed to meet nephews, nieces, and in-laws.

On each visit, I saw my mother getting older and my father getting weaker until he died. My brothers became adults overnight, and I didn't see the mornings or afternoons of their manhood. The streets had changed direction, and the buses were more crowded than before. The subway went to new locations, and the Portuguese humor had to be interpreted by my sister, and I still didn't understand it.

I remember the flight to New York in 2003 when I wrote down plans to move back to Brazil after I finished my MBA. It was mostly led by my feeling of missing the family get-togethers on Sundays and all the birthday parties. My divorce had a hand in it, too; plus, the calls on Christmas Eve were sadder than happier.

A part of me felt I wanted to give up my lovely life in Rhinebeck, New York, and move back to Brazil to help care for my mother. There's something to be said about being of service, especially when it's being of service to your mother. It would be nice to help her have a better life. But that contradicts everything I know about creation—that we create our own reality. Plus, I didn't know if I really wanted to leave New York.

When it was getting close to my time to leave Brazil again, I said goodbye to my brothers, sister, and sisters-in-law, who had been upgraded to sisters after all the "blood work" they did to help with my mother. I said a strong goodbye to my mother, who had tears in her eyes, and I promised to be back soon and help her with her future home once she was well enough to move.

As my brother, Marcus, drove me to the airport, tears ran down my face. I didn't have to be strong for my mother anymore. I felt so divided between my mother in Brazil and my life in New York. Marcus assured me that Mom would be fine. I saw the Sugar Loaf in the distance on the way to the airport. Silently, I longed for the days I used to sit by the beach and contemplate my life at the sight of two mountains that resembled a sweet loaf of bread, as called by the early Portuguese.

For the first time, I was glad that the flight from Rio to New York would be nine hours long. I would have to return to work the very next morning, and my body needed to sleep, my emotions needed to be reset, and my energy needed to be renewed. I boarded the plane and took a window seat. I used my blanket and a neck pillow to make myself comfortable. Between the sleeping and waking moments of the flight, I contemplated how to go back to Rio, work, and move my girls. I was still on the fence and had emotional strings in Rio and in Rhinebeck.

As soon as I landed, I picked up my phone messages and immediately felt overwhelmed. I even had to pull over during the drive home to participate in a conference call. As soon as I got off the conference call, my boss called to find out if I had been able to participate in the call. I wanted to say, "Yes, my mother is fine. Thanks for asking!" Maybe I needed to think twice about my job and staying in New York. Welcome home to me!

I jumped right into work. I worked from home that day late into the evening, dividing my attention between Rio, work, and living in New York. At the end of my day,

I took a long shower to clear my energy and tears that arrived every time I thought of my mother and went to bed, so I didn't have to think about anything else.

The following day, I woke up to go to work. I meditated with difficulty. I took a shower and got dressed for work. I called my children in Switzerland and my sister in Brazil. In twenty-four hours, my sister had hired a nurse, got my mother into the doctor's office for a follow-up, and learned that my mother's wounds were healing nicely.

That morning, on my way to work, I ended up in the hospital. I injured my finger when it got stuck between the panels of my garage door. The pain was unbelievable, and I was sure I had broken it. I ran cold water over it and waited a few minutes to see if the pain would subside, but it didn't. I tried to drive myself to the hospital, but the pain wouldn't let me. Luckily, my neighbor, Diane, was available to drive me.

The X-ray showed that I hadn't broken my finger. That was a relief! I was sent home with painkillers. As soon as I got home, I called my boss to tell him what had happened and that I wouldn't be going to work. I slept for the entire day.

Early in the evening, when I finally awoke rested, connected, and with a clear mind, I sat up in bed and understood the tenth wisdom that had arrived suddenly in my thoughts:

"Love is indivisible."

Wisdom comes from inside. It clicks when we make time to pay attention. Arriving in New York and running to catch up with work was not a good soul practice. My trip to the hospital was what the universe had created to force me to slow down and discover this wisdom that came out of my own experience.

I cannot weigh my love for my mother in Rio and my love for my life in New York with my children. Love cannot be divided. Love cannot be a source of division. Love encompasses *all*. The struggles I experienced traveling back to New York came when I tried to divide love instead of living love in its full form.

For my mother's entire life, she made decisions that she felt were out of love. She chose to stay with my father, to have his children, to take money from his pockets, to ask for help, to go back to work, to confront her abusive husband, to be evicted three times, to live alone, to retire but continue to work, to have an accident, and to restart her life living with her daughter. Although she might not have full awareness of the choices. Nevertheless, there is so much love in all that she went through, and if we weigh up our actions, thoughts, and emotions, love can be missed.

Love is not a two-way street to New York from Rio. Love is the way. Love is all that happens. Love is to decide to stay and to decide to go. Love is to run away and to stay put. Love is being with my mother and being with my children. Love is waking up in the night and sleeping through it. Love is writing letters and staying silent. Love is forgiving and forgetting. Love is cooking, praying, and doing laundry. Love is finding your own happiness. Love is…

My mother went to live with my sister and two of my brothers, and by 2017, she had physically recovered about 90 percent. My family felt that she was too absent-minded to live alone, even though that's what she still wanted. Her retirement fund is not enough to afford her a place of her own. She had grown a bit more accustomed to living with my siblings. For years, she spent her weekends visiting my other brothers, going on small trips, and going to church. She belonged to a senior social group that met weekly for different kinds of social activities, and that made her really happy.

I visited my mother again for her eightieth birthday in November that same year. It was a great visit, but it was not a vacation. She was happy to see me and have her children together on her birthday. She didn't remember the time I visited her after the accident or the events that happened after the accident, including donating everything during the closing of her house. I will leave it at that.

In 2022, my siblings and I made the hard decision to place her in a nursing home. My mother has dementia and is in a wheelchair. My siblings visit her weekly, and I make my way to Brazil two or three times a year. My mother doesn't know where she is, and my family reminds her multiple times during each visit. She is healthy and will turn ninety years old in November 2023.

At every daily visit to the outside patio, she is delighted by the sight of the trees. There is a mango, jackfruit, and coconut trees. She remembers her maternal grandfather, a cranky Portuguese who had a small farm with the same trees. She recalls the story of visiting him and hearing him complain about his grandchildren eating the profits.

My mother didn't want to live with his children, and she finally got her wish.

LIFE IS A JOURNEY

Women's wisdom is found everywhere. We learn it from what we do in love and from what we do in fear, regardless of our choices. Take the time to discover and make it a way of life, as the Brazilians do with rice and beans. It lives inside of you already, and everywhere you are willing to look. Your life is unfolding daily and giving you the opportunity to connect with it. Go ahead and be, do, and have your heart's desires. Have a wonderful journey.

Carta para a minha Mãe

Querida Mãe,

Obrigado por tudo que fez por mim e pelas lições que você me deu com sua vida, sua alma, e continua me dando. Espero que essas lições sejam passadas de todas mães para todas filhas; de filhas para netas e bisnetas no mundo inteiro. Desejo que a sua história seja traduzida por letras de amor e vivam transparente neste livro e no coração das mulheres que precisam se reconhecer na sua história.

Você faz parte do coração da humanidade. A sua coragem contribui para a consciência feminina – que a cada dia cresce mais claramente – de que a mulher pode tudo quando realmente quer ser, ter ou fazer o que der vontade, sem ter vergonha.

Eu te amo muito. Quero que você saiba que a sua vida é uma lição de amor infinito e sabedoria para mim. Eu espero que esteja sendo uma mãe tão maravilhosa para as minhas filhas como você foi e tem sido para mim. E se as minhas filhas tiverem por mim a metade da admiração que eu tenho por você, meu coração saberá que realmente fiz meu papel de Mãe.

Beijos,

Ana

A Letter to My Mother—Translation

Dear Mom,

Thank you for all you have done for me and for the life lessons you gave me with your life and soul and still do. I hope that these lessons will be passed from mothers to daughters and from daughters to granddaughters and great-granddaughters in the world. I wish that your story be translated through the love of these words and live transparently in the minds and hearts of the women who need to recognize themselves in your story.

You are the heart of humanity. Your courage contributes to the feminine consciousness that grows in clarity each day, cementing that women can do everything when they really want to be, have, or do what their hearts desire without feeling shame.

I love you very much. I want you to know that your life is a lesson of infinite love and wisdom to me. I hope that I'm as wonderful mother to my children as you were and are to me. And if my daughters feel half of the admiration I have for you, my heart will know that I have indeed fulfilled my role of mother.

Kisses,

Ana

Resources

RECIPES

MY MOTHER'S BRAZILIAN RICE – SERVERS 8

Ingredients:

- 2 cups white rice
- 3 tablespoons vegetable or olive oil (My mother used vegetable oil most of the time.)
- 1 onion, thinly chopped
- 3 cloves garlic, minced
- 4 cups hot water
- 1 tablespoon salt

Directions:

1. Place the rice in a colander and rinse thoroughly with cold water.
2. Add the oil to the saucepan over medium heat. Add the garlic and onion, and stir until the onion is yellow and the garlic is golden.
3. Add the rice and stir frequently until the rice begins to turn a golden color.
4. Add the hot water and salt. Add more salt to taste if you like.
5. When the water comes to a boil, lower the heat, cover the saucepan, and cook for about fifteen minutes or until the water has been fully absorbed.

MY RECIPE VARIATIONS
TO MY MOTHER'S BRAZILIAN RICE:

COCONUT RICE

- Use Basmati Rice.
- Replace the olive oil with three tablespoons of coconut oil.
- Replace the hot water with chicken stock.
- Replace salt with one tablespoon of saffron.

LEFTOVER RICE – SERVERS 8

Ingredients:

- 2 cups of cooked rice at room temperature
- 1 cup of chorizo, smoked sausage, or cubed chicken. You can use any leftover combination.
- 2 tablespoons olive oil
- ½ onion, thinly chopped
- ½ green pepper, thinly chopped
- ½ cup of tomato sauce
- ¾ cup of heavy cream
- ¾ cup of grated romano cheese
- Black pepper, red pepper, and parsley

Directions:

1. Preheat the oven to 350 degrees.
2. Add the oil to a saucepan over medium heat. Add the chorizo, sausage, or chicken, and cook until brown.

3. Add the onion and green pepper, and stir until the onion is yellow.
4. Add the tomato sauce and heavy cream and stir frequently.
5. Add the black pepper, red pepper, and parsley to taste.
6. Add the rice and half a cup of romano cheese, and cook for 2–3 minutes.
7. Transfer the mixture to a baking dish, and sprinkle the remaining grated romano cheese.
8. Bake for 20–25 minutes.

MY MOTHER'S BEANS – SERVERS 8

Ingredients:

- 1 bag (12 ounces) dry black beans or brown beans
- 4 tablespoons olive oil
- 1 large piece of chorizo or smoked sausage, cubed
- 2 bay leaves
- 1 onion, diced into ¼-inch pieces
- 4 cloves garlic
- 1 green pepper, diced into ¼-inch pieces
- 1 tomato, diced into ¼-inch pieces (Only add if you aren't going to freeze the beans.)
- Parsley
- 1 tablespoon black pepper
- 1 teaspoon cumin
- Salt to taste
- 2 tablespoons white vinegar (secret ingredient)

Directions:

1. Soak the beans for at least two hours.

2. Add two tablespoons of the olive oil to a large saucepan at medium heat.
3. Add the chorizo and cook it until it turns brown.
4. Add the presoaked beans, and cover them with water up to twice the amount of the beans.
5. Add the bay leaves.
6. When the water starts to boil, cover the pan, lower the heat, and cook for two hours.
7. In a separate saucepan, add the remaining olive oil, onion, and garlic, turning the heat to low. Cook until the onion and garlic are golden brown.
8. Add the green pepper and tomato, and cook until the vegetables are soft.
9. Add three full ladles of the cooked beans and smash them with a wooden mallet.
10. Add the black pepper, cumin, and salt to taste. Cook for ten minutes on low heat.
11. Add the onion, garlic, vegetables, and beans back to the large saucepan.
12. Add the vinegar, stir, and cook for another thirty minutes on low heat.
13. Add parsley to taste and more salt, if you like, and serve.

PS: Make it vegan by removing the chorizo.

MY BEAN SOUP – SERVERS 4

Ingredients:

* 2 cups cooked beans per the recipe above
* 2 cups chicken broth
* ¼ cup heavy cream

Directions:

1. In a medium saucepan, add the beans and chicken broth and bring them to a boil.
2. Remove the pan from the heat, and add it to a blender for one minute.
3. Return the mixture to the saucepan; add the heavy cream, stir, and serve.

MY BEET SOUP - SERVERS 4

Ingredients:

- 2 tablespoons olive or coconut oil
- 1 sweet onion, diced
- 2 cloves garlic, minced
- 6 medium beets, peeled and diced
- 2 cups chicken broth
- ¼ cup heavy cream
- Salt and pepper to taste

Directions:

1. In a medium saucepan over medium heat, add the oil, onion, and garlic. Cook until golden, stirring frequently.
2. Add the beets and the chicken broth. Add more water, if needed, to cover the beets. When it begins to boil, lower the heat and cook for 15–20 minutes until the beets are soft.
3. Remove the pan from the heat, and add the soup to a blender. Blend for one minute.
4. Return the soup to the saucepan; add the heavy cream and salt and pepper to taste. Cook for one minute and serve.

MY CAULIFLOWER SOUP - SERVERS 4

Ingredients:

- 2 tablespoons olive oil
- 1 sweet onion, diced
- 2 cloves garlic, minced
- 1 cauliflower head, cored and chopped
- 4 cups chicken broth
- 1 bay leaf
- Dash of paprika
- ¼ cup heavy cream
- Salt and pepper to taste

Directions:

1. In a medium saucepan over medium heat, add the oil, onion, and garlic. Cook until golden, stirring frequently.
2. Add the cauliflower, bay leaf, paprika, and the chicken broth. Add more water, if needed, to cover the cauliflower. When it begins to boil, lower the heat and cook for thirty minutes until soft.
3. Remove the pan from the heat, remove the bay leaf, and add the soup to a blender. Blend for one minute or less.
4. Return the soup to the saucepan; add the heavy cream and salt and pepper to taste. Cook for another minute and serve.

BRIGADEIRO (CHOCOLATE TRUFFLE) – MAKES 30 UNITS

Ingredients:

- 1 can sweetened condensed milk
- 3 tablespoons unsweetened cocoa powder
- 1 tablespoon salted butter
- ¾ cup granulated chocolate

Directions:

1. In a medium saucepan, combine the condensed milk, cocoa, and butter.
2. Cook over medium heat, stirring frequently until the mixture thickens.
3. Remove the pan from the heat, and let it cool down until you can touch it.
4. Pour the granulated chocolate on a flat plate or surface.
5. Using your hands, roll the mixture, making one-inch balls, and roll them in the granulated chocolate. Place the balls on the serving plate and enjoy!

ABOUT THE AUTHOR

Ana Barreto is a Brazilian-American Personal Development teacher, author, Feng Shui Consultant, and coach living in upstate New York. At eighteen years of age, she left her parents' traditional patriarchal home in Rio de Janeiro, Brazil, and broke the established female roles of her upbringing. Two years later, she moved to New York and began her college education.

While attending Marymount College, at that time a women-only institution, Ana began to learn about women's rights and empowerment. Her passion for women's development and growth led her to study psychology, women in history, business, leadership, meditation, spirituality, and Eastern philosophies. She holds Bachelor's and Master's degrees in Business Administration.

Since 2016, Ana began publishing books, meditations, courses, and inspirational content for women. She is the founder of the Body, Mind, and Wisdom School for Women.

Ana's purpose is to help people improve the quality of their lives. Her mission is to inspire, guide, and coach women through her books, classes, meditations, and inspirational material, helping them find their inner compass and live great lives.

When Ana isn't working or writing books, she enjoys cooking, traveling, hiking, biking, and kayaking. She also loves spending time with her partner, Jim, daughters Erica and Isabel, stepdaughters Cindy, Janet, and Christine, and her friends.

Made in the USA
Middletown, DE
02 October 2023

39942066R00124